BUILDING
VOCABULARY
SKILLS & STRATEGIES

LEVEL
6

by LORNA PECK

BUILDING VOCABULARY
SKILLS & STRATEGIES

LEVEL **3**

LEVEL **4**

LEVEL **5**

LEVEL **6** ⇦

LEVEL **7**

LEVEL **8**

Development and Production: Laurel Associates, Inc.
Cover Design: Image Quest, Inc.

SADDLEBACK
PUBLISHING·INC.
Three Watson
Irvine, CA 92618-2767

E-Mail: info@sdlback.com
Website: www.sdlback.com

ISBN 1-56254-724-0

Printed in the United States of America
10 09 08 07 06 05 04   9 8 7 6 5 4 3 2 1

CONTENTS

Welcome to
BUILDING VOCABULARY SKILLS & STRATEGIES!

We at Saddleback Publishing, Inc. are proud to introduce this important supplement to your basal language arts curriculum. Our goal in creating this series was twofold: to help on-level and below-level students build their "word power" in short incremental lessons, and to provide you, the teacher, with maximum flexibility in deciding when and how to assign these exercises.

All lessons are reproducible. That makes them ideal for homework, extra credit assignments, cooperative learning groups, or focused drill practice for selected ESL or remedial students. A quick review of the book's Table of Contents will enable you to individualize instruction according to the varied needs of your students.

Correlated to the latest research and current language arts standards in most states, the instructional design of *Building Vocabulary Skills & Strategies* is unusually comprehensive for a supplementary program. All important concepts—ranging from primary-level phonics to the nuances of connotation— are thoroughly presented from the ground up. Traditional word attack strategies and "getting meaning from context clues" are dually emphasized.

As all educators know, assessment and evaluation of student understanding and skill attainment is an ongoing process. Here again, reproducible lessons are ideal in that they can be used for both pre- and post-testing. We further suggest that you utilize the blank back of every copied worksheet for extra reinforcement of that lesson's vocabulary; spelling tests or short writing assignments are two obvious options. You can use the Scope and Sequence chart at the back of each book for recording your ongoing evaluations.

When you speak, you don't have to worry about spelling and punctuation! You do, however, have to be concerned with grammar and style.

A. Directions: Use the words and phrases in the box to complete the sentences.

emphasize	facial expressions	smirk	nonverbal	gestures	shrug
words	raising your eyebrows	frown	intonation	verbal	

1. You speak _____ out loud when you communicate orally.

2. Spoken communication is sometimes called _____ communication.

3. _____ communication does not involve speaking or writing.

4. People often make _____ with their hands and bodies when they communicate.

5. By using your eyes and mouth in certain ways, you can communicate with _____.

6. You _____ some words more than others when you are speaking.

7. If you _____ while you're speaking, you communicate disapproval.

8. The _____ of your voice is the way it rises and falls when you are speaking.

9. You can express surprise or shock by _____ while you are speaking.

10. A smug or sarcastic smile—a _____—is an effective way to express an attitude of superiority.

11. When you _____ your shoulders, it usually means you don't know or don't care.

B. Directions: Write an original sentence using each of these verbs: *stress, gesture, smirk, shrug.*

1. _____

2. _____

3. _____

4. _____

Name: _____ **Date:** _____

> Humans begin learning to speak when they are babies.
> People learn to write in kindergarten and first grade.

A. Directions: Use the words in the box to complete the sentences. Each word is used only once. Then write **T** or **F** to show whether each sentence is *true* or *false*.

spell	recognize	grammar	alphabet	punctuation	pronounce	uppercase	reading

1. _____ Writing is the "partner" of _____.

2. _____ A written word is made up of letters. To use words in oral communication, you must know how to _____ words letter by letter.

3. _____ The rules about how words go together in sentences is called _____. Most sentences have both subjects and predicates (verbs).

4. _____ The following marks are examples of _____: , " ! ? ; : . .

5. _____ Using _____ letters at the beginning of certain words is called capitalization.

6. _____ To read, you do not have to be able to sound out, or _____, the letters and words.

7. _____ All of the letters in a language make up that language's _____, and all languages use the same writing system as English.

8. _____ To read, you must be able to _____ the letters in words.

B. Directions: Circle eight examples of written communication.

books	hieroglyphics	telephone calls	declamation	fliers
lectures	Internet Web pages	term papers	magazines	gestures
mime	business letters	newspapers	business discussions	

Building Vocabulary Skills and Strategies, Level 6 • Saddleback Publishing, Inc. ©2004 • 3 Watson, Irvine, CA 92618 • Phone (888) SDL-BACK • www.sdlback.com

Name: _____ Date: _____

When you greet people, you might say "hello," "hi," or even something like "yo." Your choice of words may depend on whom you're speaking to. It can also depend on when and where you're speaking to them.

A. Directions: Circle the more formal word in each pair. That's the one you might use when speaking with your friends' parents or your boss.

1. friend / buddy

2. mother / old lady

3. bread / money

4. food / chow

5. split / leave

6. exactly! / right on!

7. fink / informer

8. police officer / cop

Sometimes formality of speech is a matter of *degree*. One word or phrase may be just slightly more formal than another. (Neither one may be slang.) More formal words tend to make you sound more *educated*.

B. Directions: Complete the less formal word in parentheses by writing in the missing letters.

1. The accident victim was **hysterical** (out of con __ __ __ l).

2. A hysterical person's speech is often not **coherent** (cl __ __ r).

3. Moe's hamburgers were always **delicious** (t __ __ ty).

4. Only two hours have **elapsed** (pa __ __ __ d) since the plane lifted off.

5. **Excessive** (Too __ __ __ __) eating usually results in weight gain.

6. **Impertinent** (Sa __ __ y) speech is not appropriate in the classroom.

7. The conversation we had was downright **insipid** (d __ __ __).

8. Dad thinks my plans for the future are too **nebulous** (v __ __ ue).

Name: _____ **Date:** _____

Slang **is used in conversation, but it is not acceptable in formal or informal writing.**

Directions: Write a letter to match each slang word or phrase with its meaning.

1. _____	**airhead**	a.	a child
2. _____	**bonkers**	b.	a Yankee; an American
3. _____	to **deck**	c.	cause problems
4. _____	**fender-bender**	d.	clothing
5. _____	to **get it**	e.	criticize or dismiss
6. _____	**hairy**	f.	cook something in the microwave oven
7. _____	**in**	g.	crazy
8. _____	**jerk**	h.	all right
9. _____	to **knock**	i.	difficult; dangerous
10. _____	to **luck out**	j.	done fast, but not very well
11. _____	to **make waves**	k.	fashionable
12. _____	to **nuke**	l.	killed
13. _____	**OK**	m.	many; countless
14. _____	**peanuts**	n.	pimple; acne
15. _____	**quick and dirty**	o.	minor car accident
16. _____	**rug rat**	p.	annoying person
17. _____	**shades**	q.	unintelligent person
18. _____	**threads**	r.	sunglasses
19. _____	**umpteen**	s.	to be lucky or fortunate
20. _____	**wasted**	t.	to hit someone
21. _____	**Yank**	u.	to understand something
22. _____	**zit**	v.	very little money

Name: _____   **Date:** _____

Did you ever wonder why you had to learn the letters of the alphabet in order? Well, just try to use a dictionary without knowing which letter comes before or after another!

A. Directions: Words defined in the dictionary are listed in alphabetical order. List the words below in alphabetical order.

preview	neutron	satisfy	antibody	glory
estimate	tangible	upbraid	motorize	likely

1. _____

2. _____

3. _____

4. _____

5. _____

6. _____

7. _____

8. _____

9. _____

10. _____

B. Directions: When you alphabetize the words in this box you'll have to check out the first *two* or *three* letters.

embody	excite	eyebrow	earache	entire
estimate	empower	ebb	eleven	edge

1. _____

2. _____

3. _____

4. _____

5. _____

6. _____

7. _____

8. _____

9. _____

10. _____

Name: _____   Date: _____

A. Directions: List the words in alphabetical order. Notice that the first *two* letters are the same in all of the words.

place	plague	pledge	plumbing	plural
playoff	plead	plank	plywood	plow

1. _____

2. _____

3. _____

4. _____

5. _____

6. _____

7. _____

8. _____

9. _____

10. _____

B. Directions: Write any word that would appear between the listed words. If you need help, check a dictionary.

1. platinum _____ plausible

2. repay _____ repent

3. father _____ fathom

4. dub _____ dud

5. shake _____ shall

6. tramp _____ tranquil

7. mope _____ morbid

8. hourglass _____ housefly

Name: _____   Date: _____

You know that there are five vowels—*a, e, i, o, u*—in the English alphabet. Did you know that each vowel can be pronounced in different ways?

Directions: Listen for the vowel sounds as you read the words in the box. Then write each word under the vowel sound you hear.

through	miss
weigh	oxen
seam	shy
pint	bunk
tough	bread
clasp	odd
shock	boat
fiddle	plaque
plead	brew
vest	creep
thigh	logo
glue	task
clothes	fresh
plate	gait
much	stitch

A SOUNDS

1. short A (lad)
   clasp

2. long A (day)

E SOUNDS

1. short E (set)

2. long E (key)

I SOUNDS

1. short I (bit)

2. long I (bite)

O SOUNDS

1. short O (top)

2. long O (row)

U SOUNDS

1. short U (pup)

2. long U (dew)

Name: _____   Date: _____

A. Directions: Say each **boldface** word aloud. Then cross out the words that do *not* have the same vowel sound.

A SOUND

1. **answer**

   law

   table

   plant

I SOUND

3. **city**

   inch

   lion

   rifle

U SOUND

5. **prune**

   bushy

   study

   ruin

E SOUND

2. **dread**

   were

   empty

   legal

O SOUND

4. **moment**

   product

   olive

   poem

B. Directions: Circle a word to correctly complete each sentence.

1. The word *bough* rhymes with the word (*trough* / *allow*).

2. The *e* in *insect* makes a (long / short) vowel sound.

3. The word *glaze* rhymes with the word (*jazz* / *plays*).

4. The *u* in the word *tuna* makes the (long / short) vowel sound.

5. The word *gown* rhymes with the word (*grown* / *noun*).

6. The *a* in the word *adjective* makes the (long / short) vowel sound.

7. The word *hear* rhymes with the word (*there* / *cheer*).

Did you know that the most common double vowels in English words are ee and oo?

Directions: Complete the following words with *ee* or *oo*. Then write an original sentence using each word.

1. d __ __ pen _____

_____

2. s __ __ the _____

_____

3. g __ __ dness _____

_____

4. s __ __ the _____

_____

5. disagr __ __ _____

_____

6. childh __ __ d _____

_____

7. misd __ __ d _____

_____

8. fr __ __ ly _____

_____

9. __ __ dles _____

_____

10. r __ __ kie _____

_____

11. wh __ __ dle _____

_____

12. pr __ __ f _____

_____

Name: _____ **Date:** _____

Directions: First, complete each **boldface** clue word with a pair of consonants from the box. Then use the clues to help you complete the crossword puzzle.

cc	dd	ll	mm	nn	pp	ss

ACROSS

4. **me __ __ le:** to interfere

5. **o __ __ ult:** having to do with mysterious powers, such as magic or astrology

6. **sa __ __ ow:** sickly looking; pale yellow

7. **su __ __ it:** the highest point

8. **Mi __ __ i __ __ i __ __ i:** a river in the U.S.

9. **Te __ __ e __ __ ee:** a state in the eastern central part of the U.S.

11. **a __ __ als:** a record of events, year by year

12. **i __ __ emorial:** from a time before anyone can remember

DOWN

1. **be __ __ igerent:** ready to fight or quarrel

2. **i __ __ ense:** very large; huge

3. **i __ __ uminate:** to make something clear; to brighten

6. **su __ __ e __ __ or:** someone who comes after another in a job, such as the presidency

7. **sate __ __ ite:** an object in orbit around a planet

10. **pa __ __ id:** without much color

Name: _____   **Date:** _____

Homographs are words that are spelled alike but have different meanings. Sometimes they have different pronunciations, too (example: the *bow* on a gift, the *bow* of a ship).

Directions: Look up these homographs in the dictionary. Notice that each word has several different meanings. Write two sentences using each homograph. Make sure to use different meanings for each word.

1. **cow** _____

_____

2. **cow** _____

_____

3. **pin** _____

_____

4. **pin** _____

_____

5. **pen** _____

_____

6. **pen** _____

_____

7. **sage** _____

_____

8. **sage** _____

_____

9. **net** _____

_____

10. **net** _____

_____

Name: _____ **Date:** _____

A. Directions: Write a letter to match the homographs in the box with their meanings. Hint: You will use most of the words more than once.

a. orange	c. yellow	e. navy	g. tan
b. blue	d. green	f. rust	

1. _____ the color of buttercups

2. _____ what some people get from lying in the sun

3. _____ a sad or depressed feeling

4. _____ very dark blue

5. _____ not yet ripe

6. _____ a nautical branch of the armed services

7. _____ a piece of fruit

8. _____ what can happen to iron

9. _____ to turn a cowhide into leather

10. _____ the sky on a clear day

11. _____ reddish-brown

12. _____ cowardly

13. _____ inexperienced; new on the job

14. _____ the color of carrots

15. _____ yellowish-brown

B. Directions: Write original sentences using any four words from the box.

1. _____

   _____

2. _____

   _____

3. _____

   _____

4. _____

   _____

Name: _____   Date: _____

> A *syllable* is part of a word spoken with a single sound of the voice. Examples: One syllable—*Ha!*; two syllables—*ho-hum*; three syllables—*brouhaha. (A brouhaha is a big fuss or commotion!)*

A. Directions: Look up the **boldface** words in the dictionary. Then rewrite the word on the line, using a dot (•) to show each syllable division. For example, the dictionary shows that the word **sachet** is divided between the **a** and the **ch**. Write it like this: **sa•chet**.

1. **browbeat** _____
2. **elapse** _____
3. **misjudge** _____

4. **spiteful** _____
5. **system** _____
6. **unique** _____

B. Directions: Read the two-syllable words listed below. Then draw a line to connect each word with its meaning.

1. **blockade**
2. **hamper**
3. **tumult**
4. **suppose**
5. **chronic**
6. **random**
7. **pewter**
8. **valor**

a. to get in the way of an activity
b. bravery
c. done without planning or choosing
d. shutting off a place to keep things from moving in or out
e. a grayish metal (a tin alloy)
f. an uproar
g. coming back again and again
h. to believe, guess, think

C. Directions: Circle only the two-syllable words in the list below. Check a dictionary if you're not sure.

| rustproof | qualify | malcontent | malign | mammal | seclude |
| exhume | video | candlestick | butchery | trademark | wheedle |

Name: _____   **Date:** _____

A. **Directions:** Look up these three-syllable words in the dictionary. Then rewrite each word on the line, using a dot (•) to show where the syllable breaks are.

1. abundant _____

2. clumsiness _____

3. millionaire _____

4. probity _____

5. synthetic _____

6. vehement _____

B. **Directions:** Draw a line to connect each **boldface** word with its meaning.

1. **biweekly**	a. to make something lively
2. **electron**	b. tall, graceful, dignified
3. **intensely**	c. fortnightly
4. **myriad**	d. very large, strong, or powerful
5. **statuesque**	e. a negatively charged particle in an atom
6. **titanic**	f. strongly, deeply, extremely
7. **fabricate**	g. a very large number of something
8. **animate**	h. make, manufacture

C. **Directions:** Circle only the three-syllable words in the list below. Check a dictionary if you're not sure.

eyeglasses	pseudonym	tarpaulin	diplomacy	glandular
providential	satchel	disbelief	aboveboard	localize

Name: _____   Date: _____

Finding words that rhyme can help to build your vocabulary!

A. Directions: Next to each **boldface** two-syllable word, there's a definition of a different two-syllable word that *rhymes* with the word shown. Use the clues to help you figure out the rhyming word. Then write the word in the crossword.

ACROSS

2. **matter**   a serving dish or an old-fashioned slang word for a record

5. **tangle**   to tear, cut, or crush severely

6. **clutter**   to speak in a quiet voice

8. **navy**   sauce made from the juice of cooked meat

9. **Chaucer**   a flying UFO, or what a cup sits on

11. **thrasher** a utensil used to whip potatoes

DOWN

1. **lobster**   a member of a gang of criminals

3. **pleasure**   valuables that are sometimes called "long-lost" or "buried"

4. **tip-off**   slang word for a bad deal, or a theft

7. **cloister**   a shellfish (the one that makes pearls)

10. **lazy**   somewhat misty or smoky

B. Directions: Use each **boldface** word in an original sentence. Check a dictionary if you're not sure of a word's meaning.

1. **beauty** _____

_____

2. **misjudge** _____

_____

3. **unique** _____

_____

Name: _____   **Date:** _____

A. Directions: Use each three-syllable word in an original sentence.
Check a dictionary if you're not sure of a word's meaning.

1. **billionaire** _____

_____

2. **creation** _____

_____

3. **primitive** _____

_____

B. Directions: Read the definitions of the **boldface** words. Then use each word to
complete one of the sentences.

WORD	MEANING	WORD	MEANING
reverence	love and respect for something	pathetic	pitiful
religious	worshipping a God or group of gods	numeral	a figure, letter, or word standing for a number
levity	lively fun or joking	president	the highest officer of a company, club, or country
edible	safe to be eaten	saturate	to soak completely through
extensive	large, widespread	ovation	long and loud applause

1. A little _____ can sometimes ease a tense situation.

2. The food that was left out overnight is not _____.

3. That scientist did _____ research for many years.

4. Maria received a standing _____ after her performance.

5. A wedding held in a church is a _____ ceremony.

6. Al Gore and George Bush ran for _____ in 2000.

7. Please _____ that sponge in the soapy water.

8. My kid brother offers _____ excuses for his behavior!

9. Good citizens show _____ during the raising of the flag.

10. The Roman _____ for 20 is XX.

Name: _____   **Date:** _____

> You probably already know that nouns name people, places, and things (e.g., boys, St. Louis, parrots).

A. Directions: In the list below, circle only the nouns that name *things* (not people or places).

adorable	hot	horse	Eiffel Tower
England	sinew	dawn	mother
vegetable	Chad	velvet	superintendent
vehicle	heavy	baby	Golden Gate Bridge

B. Directions: Write eight original sentences using nouns you circled in Part A.

1. _____

_____

2. _____

_____

3. _____

_____

4. _____

_____

5. _____

_____

6. _____

_____

7. _____

_____

8. _____

_____

Name: _____ **Date:** _____

A. Directions: In the list below, circle only the nouns that name *people* and *places*.

multimillionaire	guffaw	New Orleans	plumber
vassal	diplomat	athlete	picture
judge	bilingual	President Bush	pedagogue
Spanish	bungalow	engraving	engraver

B. Directions: Write 10 original sentences using nouns you circled in Part A.

1. _____

_____

2. _____

_____

3. _____

_____

4. _____

_____

5. _____

_____

6. _____

_____

7. _____

_____

8. _____

_____

9. _____

_____

10. _____

_____

Name: _____   **Date:** _____

A verb shows *action* (Tom *ran.*) or *being* (Tom *is* a runner.).
The main verb in a sentence is called the *predicate*.

Directions: Complete the sentences with predicates from the list. (In some sentences, the verb has more than one part. Example: He **is** always **telling** crazy jokes.)

can lend	are	behave	look	take
enjoys	do participate	are coming	is	gives

1. My next-door neighbor Jack and I _____ best friends.

2. Dr. Forrester _____ lectures about communicable diseases.

3. Angie and Doug _____ turns dissecting their frog in biology class.

4. In the lunchroom, students sometimes _____ in an unruly manner.

5. My mom _____ listening to music before going to bed at night.

6. You and your older sister _____ very much alike.

7. A broken arm _____ a fairly serious injury.

8. _____ you _____ me $20 until Friday afternoon?

9. Why _____ your cousins not _____ back to our school in the fall?

10. _____ you _____ in the same track and field events every year?

Name: _____ **Date:** _____

Verb *tense* deals with *when* an action or condition occurs. Is it happening now? Has it already happened? Or hasn't it happened yet?

A. **Directions:** Read each sentence. Decide *when* the **boldface** predicate in the sentence is taking place. Write **N** for *now (present tense)*, **P** for *past tense*, or **F** for *future tense*.

1. _____ Now **is** the time for all good people to come to the aid of their country.

2. _____ Brad **left** for school this morning without eating breakfast.

3. _____ Cecilia **will be** a sophomore next year.

4. _____ We **couldn't drive** to the game because the radiator started leaking.

5. _____ Every day we **pass** by the drugstore and donut shop.

B. **Directions:** Use the **boldface** verbs to complete the sentences. (In some sentences, the predicate has more than one part. Example: He **is** always **telling** crazy jokes.)

aspire	judged	convened	was reviled	will embarrass	will celebrate

1. Dr. Simpson _____ the essay contest last month.

2. My twin brothers _____ _____ their tenth birthday on Monday.

3. Columbus _____ _____ for insisting the world was round.

4. Many of my classmates _____ to become wealthy someday.

5. The current session of Congress _____ last January.

6. My mother _____ probably _____ me by showing everyone my baby pictures.

C. **Directions:** Write original past-tense sentences using the verbs *captured* and *replaced*.

1. _____
   _____

2. _____
   _____

Name: _____   **Date:** _____

An *adjective* is a word that describes a noun or pronoun. It often comes just before the word it describes. Example: the *black* car.

Directions: Choose 10 adjectives or adjective phrases from the box to complete the sentences.

hardest	heavy metal	centennial	horror	red, red	Victorian
Zeke's	silliest	Shakespeare	long, hot	romaine	withered

1. _____ grandmother has a crystal chandelier in her dining room.

2. Breaking that habit was the _____ thing I ever had to do.

3. The poem began, "My love is like a _____ rose."

4. The _____ summer seemed to drag on and on.

5. Fresh green vegetables, such as _____ lettuce, make great salads.

6. My folks saw a _____ house not too far from here.

7. Everyone enjoyed our town's _____ celebration.

8. Sam and Diana can't wait to see that _____ movie.

9. Are you and your sister fans of _____ music?

10. Ms. Williamson's _____ class is always very popular.

Name: _____   **Date:** _____

> An adjective used *after* some form of the verb "to be" often describes the subject of the sentence.
> Example: *August is hot*.

A. Directions: Use the words in the box to complete the sentences. Each adjective should describe the **boldface** subject of the sentence. The first one has been done for you.

terrifying
bountiful
boring
delicious
burly
sweet
disorganized
contagious

1. The **harvest** was *bountiful* _____.

2. Her **closet** was _____.

3. The **subject** was _____.

4. Their **laughter** was _____.

5. That **pastry** was _____.

6. Her **moment** of victory was _____.

7. The **wrestler** was _____.

8. Yesterday's **storm** was _____.

B. Directions: Use each adjective in an original sentence. Put the adjective *after* the verb "to be" (*am, is, are, was, were, will be*). The first one has been done for you.

1. **young** *My cousin Charlie is very young.* _____

2. **free** _____

3. **valuable** _____

4. **expensive** _____

5. **ready** _____

6. **glad** _____

Name: _____   **Date:** _____

Adverbs give more information about verbs, adjectives, and other adverbs. They tell *when, where, how, what kind,* or *how much.*

EXAMPLE: The storm raged **fiercely**.

The adverb **fiercely** modifies the verb **raged**. It tells the reader *how* the storm was raging. Many adverbs end in *-ly*.

Directions: Read the adverbs and their meanings. Use an adverb to complete each sentence.

harmoniously	in a friendly way; smoothly	**spitefully**	in a nasty or mean way
squarely	directly; exactly	**casually**	in a relaxed or informal way
randomly	not planned; by chance	**handily**	easily; without much trouble
beautifully	very well; in a beautiful way	**inadvertently**	by accident; by mistake
urgently	immediately; without delay	**radically**	very much; completely

1. Laura _____ knocked the vase off the piano.

2. The cafeteria was renovated last summer. It was changed _____!

3. An absence of conflict means that things are going along _____.

4. The principal told the teacher that Chris was _____ needed at home.

5. Frances read the story _____.

6. The job was easy. Jason took care of it _____.

7. The winning numbers are selected _____.

8. The hammer came down _____ on Chet's thumb!

9. Jan regretted speaking to her mother so _____.

10. The couple _____ strolled down the hallway.

> **Think about this sentence: I saw some *extremely* lively children in the park. *Lively* is an adjective, and the adverb *extremely* shows how lively the children were.**

A. Directions: Use the adverbs in the box to complete the sentences. Each adverb should describe the adjective that comes right after it.

very	devoutly	simply	immensely	courageously

1. Mrs. Brown said to the class, "Your essays are _____ wonderful."

2. Some of our national leaders are _____ religious.

3. During World War I, Sergeant Alvin York fought _____.

4. Cal's family was _____ proud when he graduated from high school.

5. The dancer's flowered dress is _____ colorful.

B. Directions: Use each of the following adverbs in an original sentence:
beautifully, randomly, harmoniously, urgently, radically, casually.

1. _____
_____

2. _____
_____

3. _____
_____

4. _____
_____

5. _____
_____

6. _____

Name: _____   **Date:** _____

Conjunctions are words that connect clauses, phrases, or even complete sentences. The most commonly used conjunctions are *and* and *or*.

Directions: Complete each sentence with the word or phrase that makes the most sense. Use each word or phrase only once. The first one has been done for you.

Isabel	DVD player	stepfather	interesting	burritos
videotapes	city council	fence	motorcycles	sang

1. Tony likes Italian food, but I prefer hot dogs *and* ____*burritos*____.

2. My friend Tanner has a stepmother *and* a _____.

3. Sheila bought a DVD *and* a _____.

4. The Childers brothers sell cars *and* _____.

5. Mrs. Wilson will probably call on Jan *or* _____.

6. Uncle Will gave me some CDs *and* _____.

7. Cheri and Jennifer performed for the Rotary Club *and* the _____.

8. Teresa danced *and* _____ for the crowd.

9. I have time to paint either the window frames *or* the _____.

10. Do you think math class is _____ *or* boring?

CHILDERS BROTHERS

Name: _____   **Date:** _____

It's easy to see that the words *but, if, because,* and *so* are often used as conjunctions.

A. Directions: Complete each sentence with the clause that makes the most sense. Use each group of words only once.

you missed the field trip	**she is hoarse**	**they drive all night**
no one fails the test	**she can play in the band**	**he wants to graduate**
they were extremely harsh	**he could get his GED**	

1. Chelsey wants to sing tonight, *but* _____.

2. Ed stays in school *because* _____.

3. The words you used were true, *but* _____.

4. The whole class gets an A *if* _____.

5. Yasmin practices the tambourine *so* _____.

6. Are you upset *because* _____?

7. Jamil took night classes *so* _____.

8. They can reach Boston by tomorrow *if* _____.

B. Directions: Use any words or phrases that make sense to complete the sentences.

1. The menu lists appetizers, entrees, *and* _____.

2. Hal knew the answers to the test questions, *but* _____

_____.

3. Jack asked Maria to the prom *because* _____.

4. Ken will win first prize *if* _____.

5. The faculty at Madison High is happy *because* _____

_____.

Name: _____   **Date:** _____

A *prefix* is a group of letters added to the beginning of a word to change its meaning.

You can create new words with some prefixes, such as **anti-** and **pro-**.

Anti- means "against or opposed to." **Pro-** means "for or in favor of something."

Directions: Complete each of these sentences with a word or phrase from the box.

citizenship	drugs	junk food
pollution	war	family
sports	fraud	detention

1. You are against lying, cheating, and trickery.

   You are *anti-*_____.

2. You believe that all kids should play baseball, basketball, or hockey.

   You are *pro-*_____.

3. You detest the illegal use of narcotics.

   You are *anti-*_____.

4. You think sugary or fatty foods are harmful.

   You are *anti-*_____.

5. You are in favor of loyalty among relatives.

   You are *pro-*_____.

6. You are against staying after school as a punishment.

   You are *anti-*_____.

7. You believe that all Americans should study the issues and vote.

   You are *pro-*_____.

8. You hate car exhaust that makes the air dirty.

   You are *anti-*_____.

9. You expect countries to find peaceful ways to solve their conflicts.

   You are *anti-*_____.

Name: _____   **Date:** _____

The prefix *dis-* has three meanings. Study the meanings and examples below.

EXAMPLE:

George <u>dis</u>located his shoulder.

My aunt is <u>dis</u>contented with her job.

When will bus service to Stanton be <u>dis</u>continued?

MEANING:

"away from or out of"

"the opposite of"

"to fail or refuse to do or to stop doing"

A. **Directions:** In each list, circle the definition of the **boldface** word.

1. **disarrange**

   to mess things up

   to straighten things up

   to damage a shooting gallery

2. **disassemble**

   to meet in the auditorium

   to take something apart

   to look different

3. **dishearten**

   to make someone lose hope

   to recover from a cardiac problem

   to fall out of love with someone

4. **disfavor**

   out of luck

   a feeling against something

   without party prizes

5. **discredit**

   to misplace a charge card

   to lose money

   to hurt someone's reputation

6. **dispossess**

   to legally take something away

   to put something out of the way

   to appoint deputies for a manhunt

7. **disappear**

   to cut up fruit for a salad

   to think badly of someone

   to vanish from sight

8. **disable**

   to skin a weasel-like animal

   to take away someone's ability

   to have a weakness for food

9. **disclaim**

   to refuse to accuse

   to stop digging for shellfish

   to deny

B. **Directions:** Write original sentences using three of the **boldface** words above.

1. _____

   _____

2. _____

   _____

3. _____

   _____

Name: _____   **Date:** _____

A *suffix* is a group of letters joined to the end of a word. **Suffixes** change meaning. When the **suffix** *-ing* is added to a verb, the new word can be **used as a verb, adjective, or noun.**

A. **Directions:** Complete each sentence with an **-ing** word from the box. Use each word only once.

talking	eating	sleeping	bowling	diving
dancing	offering	giving	waking	shouting

1. Break _____ is a popular entertainment on some street corners.

2. When the ambulance arrived, Jason was already _____ his son CPR.

3. Sky _____ is not my idea of safe recreation.

4. The _____ tournament lasted three days.

5. Sheila was _____ her lunch when the bell rang.

6. Why was everyone suddenly _____ so loudly?

7. That store is known for _____ good merchandise at a fair price.

8. _____ too much in class can get you into trouble.

9. Just before tests, we study every _____ moment of the day.

10. _____ is my favorite hobby!

B. **Directions:** Write original sentences using any three words from the box in Part A.

1. _____
   _____

2. _____
   _____

3. _____
   _____

Name: _____ **Date:** _____

Added to a verb, the suffix **-ate** means "to make, become, or form."

EXAMPLE: Did you valid<u>ate</u> our parking ticket? (*valid* + *ate* = to make something valid)

A. Directions: Write vowels *(a, e, i, o, u)* to complete each *-ate* word. The first one has been done for you as an example.

1. Can you v_a_l_i_date this painting as a genuine Picasso?

2. In May, the temperature fl__ct__ates between 50 and 95 degrees.

3. How can you c__nc__ntrate on your book with all this noise?

4. Theo carefully d__l__b__rated both of his options.

5. Our teacher doesn't want us to sp__c__late—she wants *facts*.

6. Our class project—a car wash—is expected to g__n__rate a lot of money.

7. It can be hard for children to s__p__rate truth from fiction in TV shows.

8. The contract st__p__lates that the repairs be finished by October 15.

The **-ize** suffix means "to make or become."   It can also mean "to act in a certain way."
(sanitize = make something sanitary)   *(fraternize = to act in a fraternal manner)*

B. Directions: Use the **boldface** words to complete the sentences.

idolize	capitalize	publicized	sympathize	personalize

1. You are supposed to _____ the first word in a sentence.

2. The important charity event needs to be widely _____.

3. Mr. Raymond suggested that I _____ my story to make it better.

4. Devoted fans often _____ popular singers and bands.

5. I _____ with you, but I don't have any money, either!

Name: _____   **Date:** _____

> Most nouns are made plural by adding -*s* or -*es*.
> But if a word ends in -*y*, the -*y* must be changed
> to -*ie* before an -*s* is added.

A. Directions: Complete each sentence with a word from the box.

batch	truth	card	report	sign
stress	box	church	egg	party

1. How many credit _____ *s* does a person need?

2. Four fundraising _____ *ies* were held to benefit the school choir.

3. I like _____ *s* cooked every way but poached.

4. You forgot to bring two _____ *es* of cookies for the bake sale.

5. After practice, the coach asked us to move 35 _____ *es* into storage.

6. Many people believe in astrological _____ *s*.

7. "We hold these _____ *s* to be self-evident. . . ."

8. The _____ *es* and strains of everyday life can be very difficult.

9. Did you know that there are 300 _____ *es* in Greensboro?

10. We used to write short _____ *s*; now we write term papers!

B. Directions: Write original sentences using three plural nouns from the sentences.

1. _____

   _____

2. _____

   _____

3. _____

   _____

Name: _____   **Date:** _____

> Did you know that the plural forms of some nouns can be very unusual?

A. Directions: Find the plural form of each **boldface** word in the dictionary. Then write it on the line. If more than one plural is acceptable, write them all.

1. **ox** _____

2. **child** _____

3. **half** _____

4. **wolf** _____

5. **calf** _____

6. **foot** _____

7. **arroyo** _____

8. **salvo** _____

9. **tornado** _____

10. **goose** _____

11. **moose** _____

12. **bison** _____

13. **mouse** _____

14. **potato** _____

15. **tomato** _____

16. **tooth** _____

B. Directions: Write original sentences using four of the plural forms from above.

1. _____

_____

2. _____

_____

3. _____

_____

4. _____

_____

Name: _____   **Date:** _____

An *abbreviation* is a shortened form of a word or phrase. We use abbreviations to save time and space.

A. **Directions:** Write the complete words represented by each **boldface** abbreviation. Check a dictionary if you need help.

1. **Supt.** _____
2. **M.C.** _____
3. **M.D.** _____
4. **P.D.** _____
5. **mg** _____
6. **ft.** _____
7. **C/O** _____
8. **Blvd.** _____

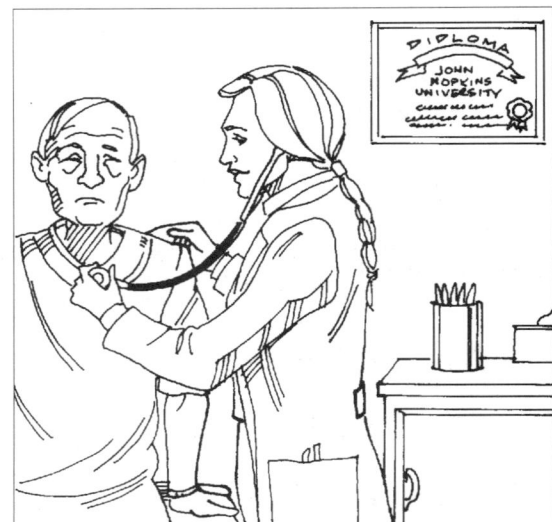

B. **Directions:** Complete the crossword puzzle. The clues are abbreviations of the answer words.

ACROSS

3. pr.
7. TD
8. chap.

DOWN

1. mi.
2. pron.
3. P.S.
4. etc. (3 words)
5. Bros.
6. Co.

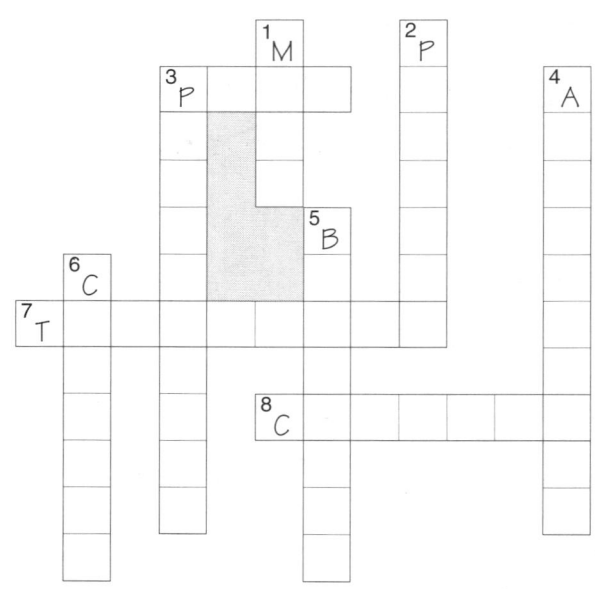

Name: _____   **Date:** _____

A. **Directions:** Write the complete name of a state next to each abbreviation.

1. **Mass.** _____
2. **Neb.** _____
3. **Conn.** _____
4. **Va.** _____
5. **Tex.** _____
6. **Nev.** _____

7. **Calif.** _____
8. **Ariz.** _____
9. **Mich.** _____
10. **Fla.** _____
11. **Ala.** _____
12. **Me.** _____

B. **Directions:** Now use the state name from Part A that correctly completes each sentence.

1. The capital of _____ was named after Abraham Lincoln.

2. The Grand Canyon is in the state of _____.

3. Many travelers go to _____ to see the Okefenokee Swamp.

4. The University of _____ is in the town of Ann Arbor.

5. Birmingham is a city in England; it is also a city in _____.

6. Reno, the "Biggest Little City in the West," is in the state of

_____.

7. The Boston Tea Party occurred in the state of _____.

8. The state of _____ borders Washington, D.C.

9. Citizens of this New England state (_____), sometimes call it "Down East."

10. _____ is known for its movie stars and earthquakes.

11. _____ has plenty of cattle ranches, oil, and dust storms.

12. _____ is home to many people who work in

nearby New York City.

Name: _____ **Date:** _____

> **An *acronym* (like TNT) is a word formed from the first letters or syllables of one or more words.**

Acronyms are usually written without periods.

EXAMPLE: GASP (Group Against Smoking in Public)

A. **Directions:** Write the acronym for each phrase.

1. _____ : Mothers Against Drunk Driving

2. _____ : self-contained underwater breathing apparatus

3. _____ : Keep it simple, silly!

4. _____ : Federal Emergency Management Agency

5. _____ : Beginner's All-Purpose Symbolic Instruction Code (hint: a programming language)

6. _____ : What you see is what you get.

7. _____ : radio detecting and ranging (hint: used by air traffic controllers)

8. _____ : severe acute respiratory syndrome

9. _____ : United Nations Educational, Scientific, and Cultural Organization

10. _____ : acquired immune deficiency syndrome

B. **Directions:** Write an original sentence using each of the following acronyms. Check a dictionary if you need help.

1. SWAK _____

_____

2. sonar _____

_____

3. SAT _____

_____

Name: _____ **Date:** _____

A. Directions: Are you up to a little challenge? To complete each sentence, replace the **boldface** word in parentheses with an abbreviation from the box.

Ms.	Maj.	Mr.	P.F.C.	Sgt.	Miss	Mrs.	Col.

1. **(Mistress)** _____ Goldman accompanied her husband to the opera.

2. **(Mister)** _____ Goldman does not like the opera, but he went anyway.

3. **(Mistress)** _____ Goldman (their single daughter) preferred to go to a pizza party.

4. **(Mistress)** _____ Goldman (a cousin) went to the movies.

5. **(Major)** _____ Simpson is hoping to get a promotion.

6. She hopes to attain the same rank as **(Colonel)** _____ Sanchez.

7. **(Sergeant)** _____ Allen is almost ready to retire.

8. **(Private First Class)** _____ Jeffers has been a soldier for one year.

B. Directions: Now let's do the reverse. In each sentence, replace the **boldface** abbreviation in parentheses with the complete title. Check a dictionary if you need help.

1. **(Pres.)** _____ Richard Nixon was in office from 1969 to 1974.

2. **(D.A.)** _____ Piper Hogan convicted 27 felons last year.

3. **(Prof.)** _____ Bert Watson teaches history at my university.

4. Do you think **(Gov.)** _____ Winfield will be reelected?

5. Where does **(Dr.)** _____ Gill practice medicine?

6. **(L.P.N.)** _____ Griffith is an emergency room nurse.

Name: _____ **Date:** _____

> *Synonyms are words with the same or nearly the same meaning. Here are some examples:* red/crimson, popular/well-liked, hated/despised.

A. Directions: Add the appropriate **boldface** word to each list of synonyms.

system	suppose	visage	aspire	recuperate	glory	complain	catastrophe	orderly

1. _____
   splendor
   beauty
   grandeur

2. _____
   disaster
   calamity
   devastation

3. _____
   face
   countenance
   expression

4. _____
   neat
   tidy
   organized

5. _____
   method
   technique
   procedure

6. _____
   recover
   convalesce
   get well

7. _____
   imagine
   pretend
   consider

8. _____
   nag
   whine
   grumble

9. _____
   seek
   desire
   aim

B. Directions: Think of synonyms for the following words. Write them on the lines. If you need help, check a dictionary or thesaurus.

1. captive (noun) / _____
2. tiny / _____
3. varied / _____
4. expel / _____
5. likely / _____
6. house / _____
7. twilight / _____
8. rational / _____
9. huge / _____
10. urgent / _____

Name: _____ **Date:** _____

A. **Directions:** Write original sentences using *synonyms* of the **boldface** words.

1. **scent:** _____

_____

_____

_____

2. **weary:** _____

_____

_____

_____

3. **spat:** _____

_____

_____

_____

4. **timetable:** _____

_____

5. **greedy:** _____

_____

6. **risky:** _____

_____

B. **Directions:** Complete the crossword puzzle. Clues are synonyms of the answer words.

ACROSS

2. nothing
4. counterfeit
5. clothe
7. untrue
8. riches
9. blaze

DOWN

1. kayak
3. rustic
5. loved
6. pace

Antonyms are words with opposite meanings. Here are some examples: *hot/cold, strong/weak, up/down.*

A. Directions: Write a letter to match each **boldface** word with its *antonym.*

1. _____ **agree**   a. enmity

2. _____ **amity**   b. prevent

3. _____ **millionaire**   c. disagree

4. _____ **cause**   d. pauper

5. _____ **mansion**   e. synthetic

6. _____ **illuminate**   f. hovel

7. _____ **kindness**   g. darken

8. _____ **natural**   h. meanness

B. Directions: Circle the *antonym* of the **boldface** word in each sentence.

1. Some people's **goodness** is quite inspiring.

   evil   sweetness   honesty

2. Riding a roller coaster can be a very **intense** experience.

   relaxing   strange   memorable

3. My dad **assembled** a kit car in less than three months.

   dismantled   refinished   analyzed

4. The doctor put my uncle on a **bland** diet.

   low-calorie   spicy   rigid

5. Many kinds of materials **contract** as they get colder.

   sweat   expand   shrink

6. When she was younger, Kiki's sister was often **clumsy**.

   fearless   awkward

   graceful

7. It takes **humility** to admit when you are wrong.

   sadness   integrity

   pride

A. Directions: Use the words in the box to make eight pairs of *antonyms*.

backward	fan	similar	independent
congenial	dawn	starved	sunset
critic	dependent	forward	sorrow
diverse	fed	joy	hostile

1. _____ / _____

2. _____ / _____

3. _____ / _____

4. _____ / _____

5. _____ / _____

6. _____ / _____

7. _____ / _____

8. _____ / _____

B. Directions: Complete the crossword puzzle with *antonyms* of the clue words.

ACROSS
2. closed
5. cheerful
7. near
8. full

DOWN
1. many
2. special
3. slow
4. skinny
6. female

A. **Directions:** Write a letter to match each **boldface** word with its *antonym*.

1. _____ **highest**   5. _____ **waste**   a. praise   e. punish

2. _____ **vassal**   6. _____ **deposit**   b. destroy   f. withdraw

3. _____ **revile**   7. _____ **fall**   c. lord   g. save

4. _____ **build**   8. _____ **reward**   d. lowest   h. rise

B. **Directions:** Circle the *antonym* of the **boldface** word in each sentence.

1. Drivers should **always** signal before they make a turn.

    never   usually   sometimes

2. Your mother seems to be an **even-tempered** person.

    good-tempered   bad-tempered

    soft-tempered

3. The restaurant manager is looking for **industrious** workers.

    lazy   hard-working   factory

4. **Enthusiasm** is a desirable quality in a cheerleader.

    liveliness   common sense

    apathy

5. **Rational** thinking is very important in a crisis.

    unrational   irrational

    negative

6. I left a **moist** towel on the kitchen counter.

    damp   moldy   dry

7. George was the rare kind of person who had no **enemies**.

    saints   friends   coworkers

Name: _____   Date: _____

A. Directions: Use the words in the box to make eight pairs of *antonyms*.

leave	catch	drought	inclusive
mirth	deluge	mellow	slob
fop	hyper	eager	return
pitch	indifferent	exclusive	sadness

1. _____ / _____

2. _____ / _____

3. _____ / _____

4. _____ / _____

5. _____ / _____

6. _____ / _____

7. _____ / _____

8. _____ / _____

B. Directions: Complete the crossword puzzle with *antonyms* of the clue words.

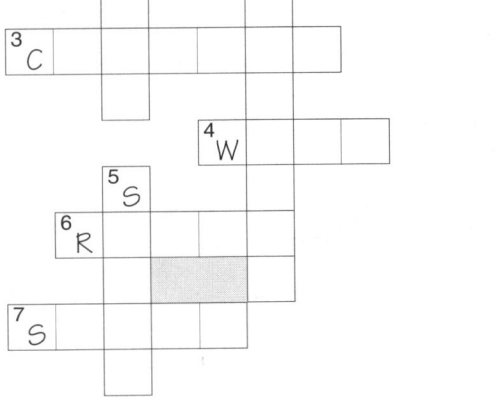

ACROSS

2. peril

3. deny

4. narrow

6. smooth

7. bitter

DOWN

1. break

2. twisted

5. drunk

Name: _____   Date: _____

> When you compare things, you find degrees of difference, such as *more* or *better*, *most* or *best*.

EXAMPLES:
- This apple is *red*. The second apple is *redder*. The third is the *reddest*.
- Candace is *relaxed*. Her sister is *more relaxed*. I'm the *most relaxed*.

In these examples, **red** and **relaxed** are adjectives. **Redder** and **more relaxed** are the *comparative* forms of the adjectives. **Reddest** and **most relaxed** are the *superlative* forms.

A. Directions: After reading each item across, write **A** next to the *adjective*, **C** next to the *comparative* form and **S** next to the *superlative* form. The first item has been done for you.

1. _A_ fast   _C_ faster   _S_ fastest
2. ____ tired   ____ most tired   ____ more tired
3. ____ thirstier   ____ thirstiest   ____ thirsty
4. ____ more willing   ____ most willing   ____ willing
5. ____ shaky   ____ shakier   ____ shakiest
6. ____ most beautiful   ____ beautiful   ____ more beautiful
7. ____ cleverer   ____ cleverest   ____ clever
8. ____ straightest   ____ straight   ____ straighter

B. Directions: Write original sentences using the **boldface** comparatives and superlatives.

1. **happier** _____

_____

2. **more boring** _____

_____

3. **most terrifying** _____

_____

4. **most organized** _____

_____

Name: _____ Date: _____

> **Comparing *related* words—words that share something in common—is one good way to achieve clear meaning. Study the example below.**

RELATED WORDS: fog, mist, sprinkle, rain, deluge

A *fog* is not as wet as *mist*. A *mist* is less moist than a *sprinkle*.
A *sprinkle* is not as wet as *rain*. A *deluge* is the *wettest* of them all.

A. Directions: Each group of **boldface** words has something in common. Rewrite the words in order of *least* to *most*. Notice that the first example is based on the size of each state. Check a dictionary if you need help.

1. Montana   *Rhode Island*
   Rhode Island   *Maryland*
   Indiana   *Indiana*
   Alaska   *Montana*
   Maryland   *Alaska*

2. brook   _____
   trickle   _____
   river   _____

3. excellent   _____
   good   _____
   OK   _____
   perfect   _____

4. small   _____
   large   _____
   medium   _____
   huge   _____
   tiny   _____

5. ocean   _____
   pond   _____
   sea   _____

6. cool   _____
   freezing   _____
   cold   _____
   chilly   _____

B. Directions: Write original sentences comparing the words in each pair.
Example: *dolphin / whale:* A dolphin is much smaller than a whale.

1. **Hawaii / the North Pole** _____

   _____

2. **hill / mountain** _____

   _____

3. **handkerchief / sandpaper** _____

   _____

Euphemisms are words or phrases that replace a word that is thought to be unpleasant or too harsh.

A. **Directions:** Circle the *euphemism* in each sentence.

1. My great-aunt (died / passed away) one year ago today.

2. A Vietnam veteran, Jim was left (visually impaired / blind) by a war wound.

3. Lena's grandmother calls herself (a senior citizen / an old person).

4. Four (janitors / maintenance engineers) work at our school.

5. Charlotte prefers not to watch movies that contain (adult / obscene) language.

B. **Directions:** Write the word from the box that matches each **boldface** euphemism. Notice that some euphemisms can be humorous!

fat	
bossy	
crippled	
died	
used	
victim	
crazy	
problem	
trounced	
use the bathroom	
quit	
dump	

1. _____ → a **disabled** person

2. _____ → a **confused** old man

3. _____ → to **break up with** a boyfriend

4. _____ → team was **defeated**

5. _____ → She **bought the farm**.

6. _____ → He is very **assertive**.

7. _____ → to **leave** a job

8. _____ → The **survivor** escaped.

9. _____ → to **powder your nose**

10. _____ → He is **overweight**.

11. _____ → She faces a **challenge**.

12. _____ → a **previously owned** car

Name: _____   **Date:** _____

Directions: Write sentences using any euphemisms you have used or read.
Circle the euphemism in each sentence.

1. _____
   _____

2. _____
   _____

3. _____
   _____

4. _____
   _____

5. _____
   _____

6. _____
   _____

7. _____
   _____

8. _____
   _____

9. _____
   _____

10. _____
    _____

Name: _____   **Date:** _____

Every night I sleep like a baby.

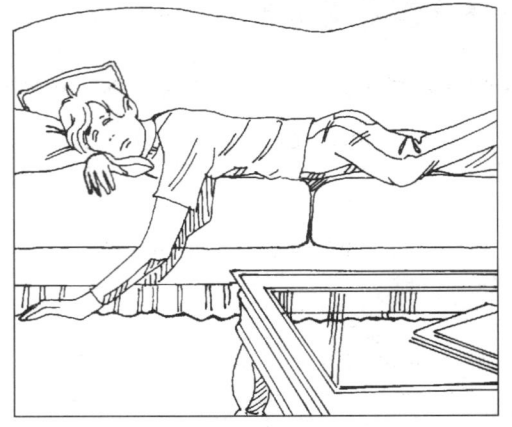

A *simile* is a comparison of two things that are *not* very much alike. Similes usually contain the words **as** or **like**.

A. Directions: Use one of the **boldface** similes to describe each person or thing. The first one has been done for you. Use each simile only once.

as grumpy as a bear	**as pretty as a picture**	**as bold as brass**
as sharp as a tack	**as giddy as a schoolgirl**	**as strong as an ox**

You might describe: Like this:

1. someone dizzy with joy   *as giddy as a schoolgirl* _____

2. a weightlifter   _____

3. someone very smart   _____

4. someone in a bad mood   _____

5. a beautiful sunset   _____

6. a daring person   _____

B. Directions: Study the sentences below. Then finish each sentence with any simile you like. Be creative. The first two have been done for you as examples.

THIS SENTENCE USES A SIMILE: When I swim, I sink like a rock.

THIS SENTENCE DOES *NOT* USE A SIMILE: When I swim, I sink, like my friend Irma does.

1. Hal is as clumsy as _*a bull in a china shop*_____.

2. Sid's cousin Ernie walks like _*he has ants in his pants*_____.

3. Dad's anger was like _____.

4. Trying to write a poem is like _____.

5. Going to the dentist is like _____.

Name: _____   **Date:** _____

A. Directions: Complete each sentence with a simile. You can use well-known similes or create new ones.

1. It seemed that she was as _____ as _____ .

2. Mr. Fitzhugh looked as _____ as _____ .

3. Denny's new car is as _____ as _____ .

4. Gil's ex-girlfriend is as _____ as _____ .

5. At my new job, the work is as _____ as _____ .

B. Directions: Use the words from the box to complete each simile.

a wet hen
a gorilla
a cat on a hot tin roof
an eel
a lamb
a kitten

1. as mad as _____
2. as uncomfortable as _____
3. as slippery as _____
4. as hairy as _____
5. as playful as _____
6. as meek as _____

C. Directions: Write original sentences using any two of these similes:

- like a cold October night
- like dew on the morning grass
- like a man without a country
- like a visit to a haunted house

1. _____

2. _____

Name: _____ **Date:** _____

The difference between *red* and *green* is obvious. The difference between *fire-engine red* and *brick red* is not so obvious—it's *subtle*. A subtle variation is a *small difference.*

Synonyms often have minor differences. For instance, the words **pleasant** and **pleasing** both mean "enjoyable." **Pleasant** suggests the good feeling a person has about something. **Pleasing** suggests the ability to cause a pleasant feeling in someone else.

A. Directions: The words in each group have similar meanings. Circle the two words in each group whose similar meanings have subtle differences. The first group as been done for you. Check the dictionary if you're not sure.

1. (push)	2. meadow	3. walk	4. help	5. despise
move	rustic	stroll	assist	harm
(shove)	rural	jog	manage	injure

B. Directions: Circle the word(s) that give(s) the sentence the correct subtle meaning. Check a dictionary to be sure.

1. Aunt Vera was (angry / furious). She threw a vase across the room!

2. Sylvia (owns / possesses) amazing psychic ability.

3. Benny is a good leader—he (governs / rules) the student council in a democratic way.

4. I (wanted to / wished I could) ride on the next space shuttle trip.

C. Directions: Use each of these synonyms in an original sentence. Be sure that your sentences demonstrate the subtle differences between the words.

1. **cheap** _____

_____

2. **inexpensive** _____

_____

Name: _____   **Date:** _____

A. Directions: Write a letter to answer each question. Use each letter only once.

a. **dictator**   d. **fortune teller**   g. **limp**   j. **dusty road**

b. **homeless**   e. **walk**   h. **manager**   k. **weather forecaster**

c. **attainable**   f. **president**   i. **improbable**   l. **antique**

1. _____ Who *foretells* things?

2. _____ Who *predicts* things?

3. _____ Who *rules*?

4. _____ Who *governs*?

5. _____ What describes many of our *wishes*?

6. _____ What describes many of our *wants*?

7. _____ What might be called *rural*?

8. _____ What might be called *rustic*?

9. _____ How do you get from one room to another?

10. _____ How might you walk if you hurt your foot?

11. _____ Whom might you *help*?

12. _____ Whom might you *assist*?

B. Directions: Use *synonyms* of the **boldface** words to complete the crossword puzzle.

ACROSS

4. They found a **significant** message on the table.

5. Earlene will come home after a **short** meeting at school.

7. The air in Arizona is quite **arid**.

8. The principal will **allow** us to use this meeting room.

9. Edward can **stare** at the stars for hours at a time.

DOWN

1. In the warm room, the ice **thawed** quickly.

2. There were **numerous** reporters in the courtroom.

3. My parents **ban** smoking in their house and car.

4. We prepared a **detailed** list of what to buy.

6. The firefighters tried to save the **blazing** house.

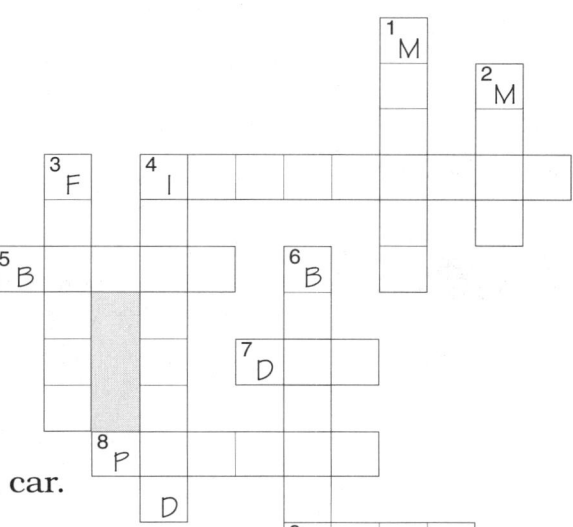

There are many ways to classify words. One way is by pronunciation. This means grouping words that sound alike or have similar vowel or consonant features.

A. Directions: Find two words in the box that rhyme with each listed word. Write them on the lines. Hint: You will *not* use all the words in the box.

prim	hesitate
align	fulfill
off	divine
pupil	confiscate
train	whey
weigh	chocolate
enough	meditation
gym	imitation
reign	phlegm
thrill	trough

1. **stay** _____ _____

2. **malign** _____ _____

3. **swill** _____ _____

4. **ovation** _____ _____

5. **percolate** _____ _____

6. **cough** _____ _____

7. **whim** _____ _____

8. **plane** _____ _____

B. Directions: Circle each word that contains the vowel *sound* you hear in **mole**.

open	tough	bow	how	whole
allow	hop	hope	dough	poll
doll	cold	suppose	posture	hallow

C. Directions: List three words that contain the vowel *sound* in each **boldface** word.

1. **eight**

2. **pave**

3. **bill**

_____   _____   _____

_____   _____   _____

_____   _____   _____

Name: _____   Date: _____

> A *consonant cluster* is two or more consonant sounds blended in the same syllable. Study the example below.

EXAMPLE: In the word **strong**, the **s, t,** and **r** sounds are clustered, or grouped together. In the word **light**, there are no consonant clusters because the letters **g** and **h** are silent. And in the work **shake**, the **s** and **h** are *not* a consonant cluster. Those letters form a new sound (**sh**) rather than being pronounced individually.

A. Directions: First, cross out words that do *not* contain a consonant cluster. Then draw a circle around the consonant clusters in the remaining words.

1. pride	4. shoe	7. align	10. straight
2. reign	5. collide	8. crisp	11. shallow
3. fright	6. might	9. jury	12. quaint

B. Directions: Use the clues to complete the crossword puzzle. Answer words all end in the **d** sound.

ACROSS

3. ownership mark made on cattle

4. a cloth pattern with colored bands and lines crossing each other

6. a strong desire for more than you need

7. a thick string or thin rope

8. the opposite of narrow

9. finish

DOWN

1. to exchange

2. spoke

4. a street procession

5. what you plant to grow something

Name: _____

Date: _____

Another way to organize words is to classify them by category.

A. Directions: Write a letter to identify the category that correctly labels each group of words. The first one has been done for you. Hint: You will *not* use all the categories.

1. __b__ cougar, koala, mallard
2. _____ mango, kiwi, papaya
3. _____ asphalt, unhappy, wishful
4. _____ digit, clavicle, diaphragm
5. _____ spoon, filing cabinet, jack
6. _____ stubborn, pensive, articulate
7. _____ globe, moon, happy face
8. _____ water, milk, tears
9. _____ scooter, van, sedan
10. _____ teepee, condominium, igloo
11. _____ glazier, teamster, longshoreman
12. _____ stop sign, blood, cardinal

a. **liquids**
b. **animals**
c. **fruits**
d. **vegetables**
e. **dwellings**
f. **types of rivers**
g. **body parts**
h. **vehicles**
i. **shape**
j. **color**
k. **number of letters**
l. **made of metal**
m. **made of wood**
n. **clothing**
o. **occupations**
p. **describe people**

B. Directions: Write examples of three things that would fit in each category. The first one has been done for you.

1. **old**   *great-grandfather*   *antique*   *fossil*
2. **wooden**   _____ _____ _____
3. **sweet**   _____ _____ _____
4. **beverage**   _____ _____ _____
5. **high (tall)** _____ _____ _____

Name: _____   **Date:** _____

A. Directions: Each group of words has something in common. Name each category as specifically as you can. For example: **apple, orange, pear,** and **apricot** are all *fruits*. To be more specific, they are all *tree* fruits (unlike strawberries or grapes, for example). The first one has been done for you.

WORDS	CATEGORY
1. four, twelve, forty, ninety-six	*even numbers*
2. pit, well, grave, trench	
3. star, asteroid, planet, moon	
4. mauve, ocher, sienna, indigo	
5. rejoice, have fun, party, enjoy	
6. steamer, monorail, gondola, dirigible	
7. comic, joke, humor, comedy	
8. boxwood, myrtle, oleander, lilac	
9. depressed, dejected, demoralized, desolate	
10. quill, marker, ballpoint, highlighter	

B. Directions: Write a category label. Then write three words that fit in that group. The first one has been done for you.

1. *WEATHER*
   storm
   lightning
   tornado

2. _____

3. _____

4. _____

5. _____

"I vote no, and I am *unanimous* about that!" Oops!
The speaker has chosen the wrong word. *Adamant*
would have been the right word to use in that sentence.

Everyone makes a mistaken word choice now and then. For example, if you say
cinnamon when you mean **synonym**, it can be pretty funny. There's a special word
for such mispronunciations or mistakes: *malapropisms*.

A. Directions: Circle the **boldface** word that correctly completes each sentence.

1. The windshield of a clean car is
(**transparent** / **translucent**).

2. When she broke her arm, Jeanette went
to see a (**physician** / **physicist**).

3. Are you (**inferring** / **implying**) that
I should go home early?

4. The Arctic explorers packed plenty of
(**pelican** / **pemmican**) to eat.

5. When did the southern states begin to
(**secede** / **succeed**) from the Union?

6. Achievers struggle hard to (**obtain** / **attain**) their goals in life.

B. Directions: The **boldface** word in each sentence is the wrong word—by just one or two
letters. In each word, the incorrect letter or letters are underlined. Use one of
the letters in the box to change the spelling when you rewrite the word on the
line. The first one has been done for you.

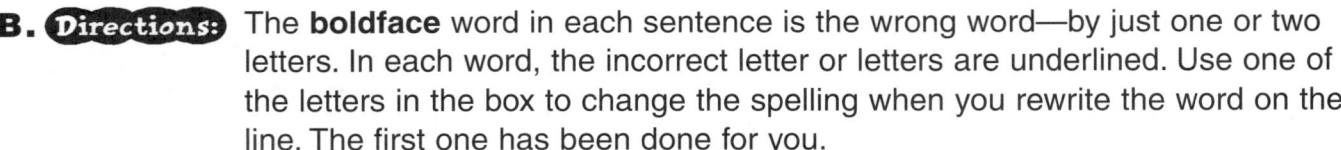

c	m	s	u	w	x	y

1. The detective is trying to **h<u>o</u>ne** in on the guilty person. _____*home*_____

2. As her boyfriend approached, Betty noticed a **glea<u>n</u>** in his eye. _____

3. Someone who has a very ambitious goal has a long **ro<u>ad</u>** to hoe! _____

4. Let's get down to the **cru<u>tc</u>h** of the matter. _____

5. "Don't" is a common **contra<u>p</u>tion**. _____

Name: _____ **Date:** _____

Directions: Notice the **boldface** malapropism in each sentence. Then write a letter to indicate the word in the box that makes sense in each sentence.

1. __l__ In western movies, the **calvary** often rescues the settlers.

2. _____ I think I'll order Boston cream pie for **desert**.

3. _____ Letitia has **expirations** to go to college someday.

4. _____ The pledge of allegiance includes the words, ". . . one nation, under God, **invisible** . . ."

5. _____ Charles works for that import-**outport** bank.

6. _____ You forgot? Let me **refurbish** your memory.

7. _____ They did a good job and deserve some **credos**.

8. _____ How can you separate the wheat from the **shaft**?

9. _____ That's a problem that needs **solutioning**.

10. _____ They're taking a **laxadaisical** attitude toward their problem.

11. _____ He turns a blind **ear** to his son's misbehavior.

12. _____ Their pool has too much of that green **allergy**.

13. _____ It sounds like you've just solved the **solution**.

14. _____ You learn to **pronunciate** a word by hearing it.

15. _____ Those injured athletes are **disgusting** their various ailments.

16. _____ Voting was to be done by secret **ballad**.

17. _____ Arthur has got one of those **sight-seeing** dogs.

18. _____ I've heard that all is **fear** in love and war.

19. _____ Much of the government's work is done by civil **serpents**.

20. _____ There will be no more discussion. It's a **dumb** deal!

a. **aspirations**

b. **export**

c. **lackadaisical**

d. **chaff**

e. **ballot**

f. **Seeing Eye**

g. **fair**

h. **done**

i. **refresh**

j. **indivisible**

k. **credit**

l. **cavalry**

m. **pronounce**

n. **servants**

o. **eye**

p. **algae**

q. **discussing**

r. **solving**

s. **dessert**

t. **problem**

Name: _____   Date: _____

A *contraction* is a shortened form of a phrase, such as *we're* (we are). Contractions are not used in formal writing. Some contractions are not used at all in written English.

To make a contraction, you put two words together. One or more letters are left out of the second word. An apostrophe (') appears in place of the missing letter or letters.

EXAMPLE: we + are = **we're**

A. **Directions:** Circle the contraction(s) in each sentence.

1. I guess we should've known better.

2. How can you say that you don't want a new car!

3. Mr. Shepherd's the new football coach.

4. If you don't hurry, you won't get there on time.

5. I'm really pleased that you've decided to stay.

6. If Gene'll only pay attention, he'll get better grades.

7. Chandler should've known better than to skip school.

B. **Directions:** Write the two complete words that are combined in each contraction. The first one has been done for you.

1. **We're** going to the lake this afternoon. _____*We are*_____

2. **I'd** go with you if I could, but I have other plans. _____

3. **Sherri's** got a new CD player. _____

4. The **judge'll** decide soon. _____

5. That tall **sheriff's** got a new badge. _____

6. The **deputy's** our new Little League coach. _____

7. **They've** never been to Denver until now. _____

8. Before last year, **they'd** always lived in Dallas. _____

9. The class **didn't** understand the instructions. _____

10. **I'm** not sure I understood them, either. _____

Name: _____   **Date:** _____

A. Directions: Write the contractions of the **boldface** words on the line.

1. **He had** _____ better get home on time!

2. He **should not** _____ stay out so late.

3. **I have** _____ got no money for a movie.

4. My **friends will** _____ loan me some.

5. **Jonah has** _____ got a very bad cold.

6. He **must have** _____ caught it from Lou.

7. **She is** _____ afraid of ghosts.

8. **I will** _____ walk through the haunted house with her.

B. Directions: Write original sentences using the **boldface** phrases.

1. **we'll** _____

_____

2. **Sophia hasn't** _____

_____

3. **James and I haven't** _____

_____

4. **Mr. Franks isn't** _____

_____

5. **you don't** _____

_____

6. **I shouldn't** _____

_____

7. **why can't they** _____

_____

8. **Bob and Alice won't** _____

_____

Name: _____   **Date:** _____

"The car is in the GARAGE." Whoa! The word GARAGE should *not* be written in capital letters!

There are lots of ways a word can be "wrong." It might be misspelled or incorrectly capitalized. It might even have the wrong meaning for the context.

A. Directions: What's wrong with each **boldface** word? First, figure out the problem. Then rewrite the word correctly. The first one has been done for you.

1. My car is so good it can **start** _____*stop*_____ on a dime.

2. Steve's bedroom door is not **plum** _____; it's crooked.

3. Does a mallard **quak** _____ the same as other ducks?

4. **strangers** _____ are not allowed on the school grounds.

5. My friend **vicki** _____ lives in Dallas, Texas.

6. I want only **halve** _____ an apple, thank you.

7. Choose a poem, memorize it, and **resite** _____ it in class tomorrow.

8. Bring in the **clown's** _____.

B. Directions: To complete the crossword puzzle, write the *correct* form of each **boldface** clue word.

ACROSS

2. My dad has a 12-foot **latter**.

5. On a cold morning, let your engine **idol** for a while.

6. The child said she had an upset **tummie**.

7. Forest **strangers** take care of national parks.

8. **Spitefull** behavior is always unpleasant.

DOWN

1. Listening is the best way to learn to **pronunciate** words.

3. **Preshus** gems are usually very costly.

4. Annette plays the **symbols** in the marching band.

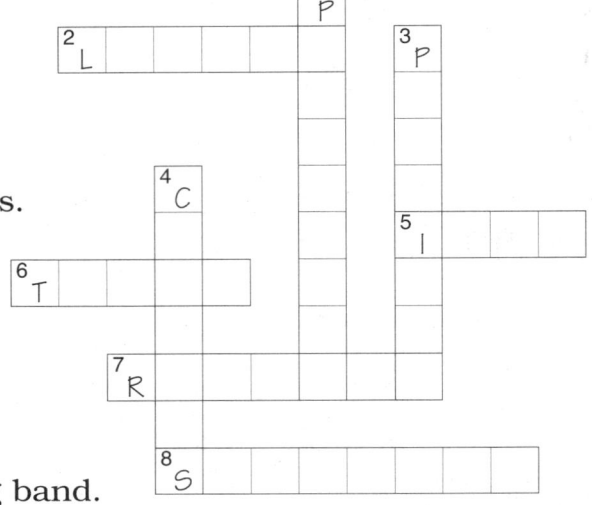

Name: _____   **Date:** _____

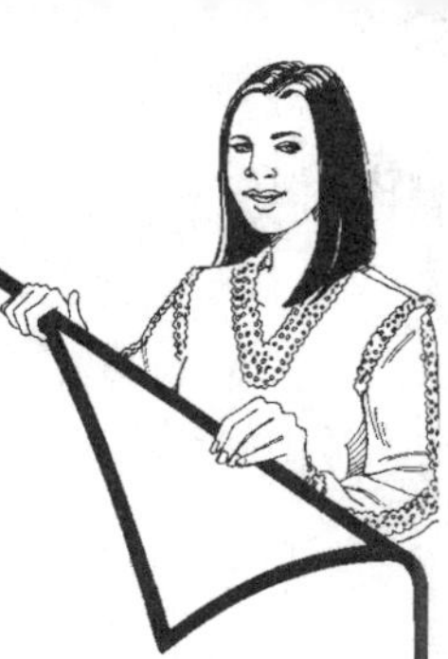

WHAT'S WRONG WITH THIS SENTENCE?

"In birds the trees are." Pardon me? That sentence should read "Birds are in the trees." Your job is to arrange the words in the proper order.

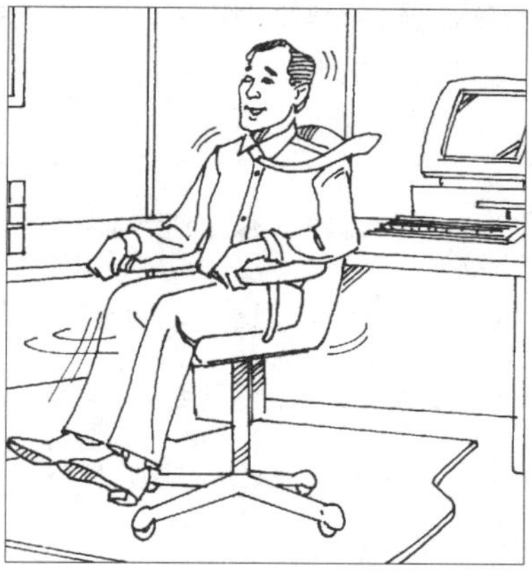

Directions: The words in these sentences are all jumbled up.

EXAMPLE: cat rat The chased the.

➜ The cat chased the rat.

Rewrite each sentence correctly. (Hint: The first word in every sentence begins with a capital letter.) The first one has been done for you.

1. dessert my is Cheesecake favorite.
   Cheesecake is my favorite dessert.
2. driveway your Please motorcycle the park in.
   ____
3. men Middle turbans East the in wear Some.
   ____
4. switchboard used operate to grandmother a My.
   ____
5. ankle accident Brad's swollen after very the was.
   ____
6. chairs use desks swivel their people Many at.
   ____
7. remains relic past is A that from something the.
   ____
8. a be to relief such home long after trip a It's.
   ____
9. impasse argument Our reached an finally.
   ____
10. not sport is taught of schools at fencing many The.
    ____

Name: ______________________________ **Date:** ______________

If the sentences in a paragraph are out of order, the paragraph may not make any sense! Logic and common sense can help you figure out correct sentence order.

A. Directions: Most paragraphs contain clue words that suggest sentence order. Read the sentence pairs below. To make sense, the second sentence has to come after the first. Circle the word or phrase in the second sentence that points back to something in the first. The first one has been done for you.

1. I like <u>apples and bananas</u>. (Those fruits) are available all year long.

2. <u>Ms. Applegate</u> lives in Fresno, California. She is a lawyer.

3. <u>Shoes</u> are very expensive at this store. I can't afford them.

4. You should go to the new <u>amusement park</u>. I went there last Saturday.

5. <u>The movie</u> Darryl saw last Saturday was a thriller. It was very exciting.

B. Directions: Sometimes the sentences in a paragraph describe steps in a process. Figure out which step comes first in each pair of sentences. Write **1** next to the first step; write **2** next to the second step. The first one has been done for you.

1. _2_ Start the car.
   _1_ Put the key into the ignition.

2. ____ Prepare the ingredients.
   ____ Cook the ingredients.

3. ____ Model the vase.
   ____ Buy the clay.

4. ____ Read the story.
   ____ Write the summary.

5. ____ Develop the film.
   ____ Take the pictures.

6. ____ Staple the pages.
   ____ Assemble the pages.

C. Directions: Write **C** for *correct* if the sentence order makes sense. Write **I** for *incorrect* if the sentences are out of order. The first one has been done for you.

1. _I_ If you see a bird, raise your hand. Let's all look for birds.

2. ____ To buy something, you need money. To get money, you must work.

3. ____ To store grain, you need a grain elevator. We can't store our grain.

4. ____ I tightened the faucet. The faucet stopped leaking.

5. ____ I tightened the faucet. The faucet was leaking.

Name: _____   **Date:** _____

Directions: Rewrite the paragraph, putting the sentences in proper order.
(Hint: Each correct first sentence has been underlined.)

1. The weather there is harsh in the winter. She lives in Buffalo, New York. <u>I have an aunt named Elvira.</u>

_____

_____

2. Unfortunately, his grades in those subjects were poor. To do that, he had to do well in math, drawing, and science. <u>Dave wanted to be an architect.</u>

_____

_____

_____

3. Cook the rice and cabbage leaves. <u>This is the recipe for stuffed cabbage:</u> Bake in the oven. Combine the cooked rice with the hamburger. Cover the stuffed cabbage with tomato sauce. Wrap the combination in the cabbage leaves. Purchase some cabbage, rice, hamburger, and tomato sauce.

_____

_____

_____

_____

_____

4. The more brain power you have, the more confidence you have. The more words you know, the more brain power you have. The more confidence you have, the better your life will be. <u>Why learn new words?</u>

_____

_____

_____

_____

Name: _____   **Date:** _____

> Some words and phrases have special meanings. They aren't meant to be taken literally. Study the example below. Such words and phrases are called _idioms_.

EXAMPLE: To have something "on hand" doesn't mean that something is actually on your hand. It means that something is ready or available.

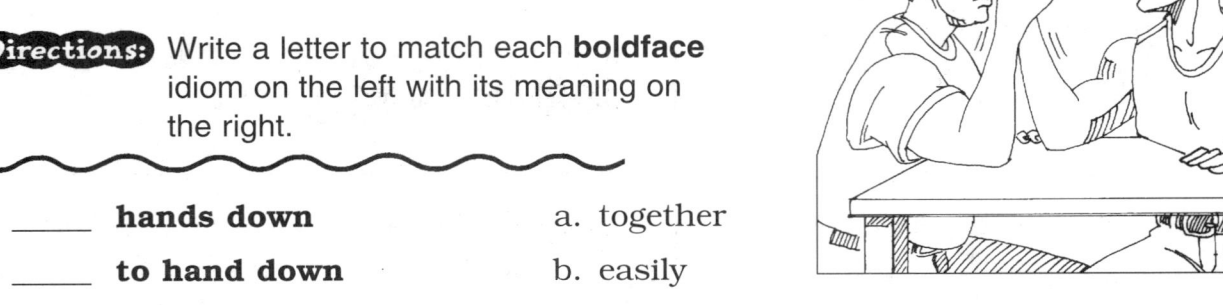

A. Directions: Write a letter to match each **boldface** idiom on the left with its meaning on the right.

1. _____ **hands down**

2. _____ **to hand down**

3. _____ **to wash one's hands of**

4. _____ **to change hands**

5. _____ **hand in hand**

6. _____ **live from hand to mouth**

7. _____ **at the hand of**

a. together

b. easily

c. to get a new owner

d. with nothing left over for future needs

e. to refuse to have anything to do with something

f. to pass something along (as from mother to daughter)

g. through the actions of

B. Directions: Circle a letter to show the meaning of the **boldface** "hand" idiom.

1. After singing, Greta got a big **hand** from the crowd.
   a. applause   b. boos   c. escorted off the stage

2. Louis Garcia is the candidate's **right-hand man**.
   a. bodyguard   b. mentor   c. closest assistant

3. I'm tired. **On the other hand**, I'd like to see that movie.
   a. from another point of view   b. from the front   c. consequently

4. Mrs. Patton's shiftless son always **has his hand out**.
   a. can't see very well   b. begs for money   c. needs a cane

5. That company is bringing in money **hand over fist**.
   a. making big profits   b. rudely grabbing   c. selling handmade goods

Name: _____   **Date:** _____

Directions: Circle the "hold" idiom that correctly completes each sentence.

1. Yasmin has (held up / held down) the same job for almost two years.

2. His court case was put (on hold / hold on) until more evidence could be collected.

3. "(On hold / Hold on) there!" the man shouted at the fleeing shoplifter.

4. The four-car accident will probably (holdup / hold up) traffic for hours.

5. Miss Withers witnessed a (holdup / hold up) at the bank yesterday!

6. The striking workers are (holding out / holding off) for more money.

7. In that movie, some soldiers (held out / held off) the enemy for 55 days.

8. At the funeral, the students (held back / held down) their tears as long as they could.

9. The boring speaker (held off / held forth) for more than an hour.

10. The circus was so popular it was (held over / held back) for another week.

Name: _____   **Date:** _____

Keep your head! Remember that idioms *aren't* meant to be taken literally.

A. **Directions:** Write a letter to match each **boldface** idiom with its meaning.

1. _____ **come to a head**

2. _____ **go to your head**

3. _____ **keep your head**

4. _____ **lose your head**

5. _____ **make headway**

6. _____ **put your heads together**

7. _____ **out of your head**

8. _____ **over your head**

a. to discuss plans with someone else

b. to be crazy or enraged

c. to reach a crisis or turning point

d. to make progress or move ahead

e. to lose control over yourself

f. to be too hard for you to understand

g. to make you feel too proud or vain

h. to maintain self-control

B. **Directions:** Circle a letter to show a meaning or example of the **boldface** idiom.

1. The big black horse won the race by a **head**.

   a. by being ahead

   b. by being smart

   c. by the length of a horse's head

2. In American history class, Maxine is **head and shoulders above** all of us.

   a. 9 inches taller

   b. a lot better than

   c. sits on a tall stool

3. The posse will attempt to **head off** the escaping bank robber.

   a. outwit

   b. turn toward

   c. surround and stop

4. The girls' basketball team is **heading for** the court right now.

   a. going toward

   b. protesting

   c. cheering for

5. Wilma tries to tackle her problems **head-on**.

   a. eventually

   b. directly

   c. indirectly

Name: _____

Date: _____

Directions: Complete each sentence with a **boldface** idiom or "hair" word from the box. Use each boldface word or phrase only once.

hairpin	hair-raising	hairspring	let your hair down	hairy
hairpiece	split hairs	hairline	hairsbreadth	hairdo

1. Don't be so nervous, Gena. Just _____ and tell us what's going on!

2. We can argue and _____ for hours, but it won't help us finish the project.

3. The speed skater won by a _____.

4. The repairman needs a tiny _____ to repair the watch.

5. Unfortunately, my father has developed a receding _____.

6. If he becomes bald on top, Dad may decide to buy a _____.

7. We experienced some _____ moments on the roller coaster.

8. Jeff drove much too fast around that _____ curve.

9. Roberta likes to change her _____ every week.

10. That horror movie has many _____ scenes in it.

Name: _____   **Date:** _____

Don't pass up this chance to show what you know about idioms!

A. **Directions:** Write a letter to match each **boldface** idiom with its meaning.

1. _____ **bring to pass**

2. _____ **come to pass**

3. _____ **pass away**

4. _____ **pass off**

5. _____ **pass out**

6. _____ **pass out**

7. _____ **pass over**

8. _____ **pass up**

a. to faint

b. to happen

c. to ignore; to leave out

d. to give out; to distribute

e. to make happen

f. to come to an end; to die

g. to falsely present something as being true

h. to refuse something or let something go by

B. **Directions:** Complete each sentence with a **boldface** idiom from the box. Hint: You will *not* use all the idioms.

came to pass
passed away
passed off
passed out
passed over
passed up
brought to pass

1. Rafael, I can't believe you _____ such a wonderful opportunity!

2. After the war, it _____ that former enemies became friends.

3. My cousin was _____ for promotion again this year.

4. Nathan nearly _____ from hunger and heat exhaustion.

5. After a long illness, Henry's great uncle _____ .

Name: _____   **Date:** _____

Directions: Complete each sentence with a **boldface** idiom from the box.
Hint: You will use two of the idioms twice.

stand in for	stand for	stand off	stand up to
stand a chance	stand by	stand up	stand out

1. Paul isn't the kind of guy who would _____

   his date.

2. If you didn't study last night, you don't _____

   on today's test.

3. Jillian's beautiful face would _____ in any crowd!

4. When Ed sees bullies bothering anyone, he's not afraid to

   _____ them.

5. If Willie gets into trouble, his brothers are always ready and willing to

   _____ him.

6. Your evidence is too weak to _____ in court.

7. If the star of the play gets sick, her understudy will

   _____ her.

8. We're about to start the TV broadcast—please _____

   for just a moment.

9. What are your beliefs? What principles do you _____?

10. The movie star told the reporters to _____ and

    stop bothering her.

Remember that the words in idioms don't carry their usual meanings.

A. **Directions:** Write a letter to match each **boldface** idiom with its meaning.

1. _____ **pull someone's leg**

2. _____ **pull down**

3. _____ **pull for**

4. _____ **pull yourself together**

5. _____ **pull off**

6. _____ **pull over**

7. _____ **pull through**

8. _____ **pull up to**

a. to manage to do something difficult

b. to safely pass through an illness or time of trouble

c. to drive to a certain place or spot

d. to fool or joke with someone

e. to get a certain salary

f. to drive a car to the curb

g. to hope for someone's success

h. to gather your courage and self-control

B. **Directions:** Complete each sentence with the correct **boldface** idiom from the box.

pull over
pull your leg
pull through
pull off
pull for

1. If you think you can _____ that trick, go ahead and try.

2. When I saw the police car's flashing red lights, I started to _____.

3. If you run for class secretary, we will all _____ you.

4. Lenny was gravely ill, but the doctor says that he'll _____.

5. Don't let those kids _____; they're just teasing you.

Name: _____   **Date:** _____

Directions: Circle a letter to show the meaning of each **boldface** idiom.

1. The troops were ordered to **fall back** about 500 yards.

   a. stumble   b. retreat   c. faint

2. Be careful not to **fall behind** in your homework.

   a. fail to keep up with

   b. put off doing

   c. refuse to do

3. I've heard some bad jokes, but yours really **falls flat**!

   a. has no air

   b. makes sense

   c. isn't funny

4. Last year Cheryl really **fell for** a guy from Chicago.

   a. liked a lot

   b. was fooled by

   c. rejected

5. The sergeant ordered the recruits to **fall in**.

   a. lie down

   b. tackle each other

   c. get in a line

6. Unfortunately, our plan to buy a new car **fell through**.

   a. was successful

   b. didn't work out

   c. was finished

7. Cookie sales usually **fall off** in the last weeks of the campaign.

   a. increase   b. dwindle   c. stop

8. It's really sad when two good friends **fall out** with each other.

   a. have a fight

   b. accidentally meet

   c. disagree

9. Every Saturday it **falls on me** to do the dinner dishes.

   a. hits me hard

   b. takes a tumble

   c. is my duty

10. At a new school, it takes a while to **fall in with** a group of friends.

    a. have a fight

    b. meet and join

    c. avoid

Name: _____   Date: _____

Are you up to date on your "shopping mall" vocabulary?

Directions: Unscramble the words that match the definitions. Then use the unscrambled words to complete the crossword puzzle. Clue 4-Across has been done for you.

ACROSS

4. *parking lot* where you leave your car at
(GARKPIN TLO) the mall (two words)

6. _____ an open space in the mall,
(RUMATI) usually two or more stories high, sometimes having a glass roof

8. _____ to stroll through the mall,
(DIWWON PHOS) just looking at the merchandise in the windows (two words)

9. _____ the person who waits on you
(SLESA RELCK) in a store (two words)

11. _____ to buy something at a store
(CRASPUHE)

14. _____ a water feature at many
(TOINFAUN) malls

15. _____ what teenagers often do at
(GNAH UTO) a mall (two words)

16. _____ where you can get your hair
(TAUBYE PHOS) done at the mall (two words)

DOWN

1. _____ the person in charge of
(GRAMANE) running a store

2. _____ another term for a group
(SPIPOGHN of stores (two words)
TRECEN)

3. _____ what you do in a store when
(WROBES) you're not sure what you want

5. _____ an area with tables and chairs,
(DOFO TORUC) surrounded by fast-food restaurants (two words)

7. _____ things a store has for sale
(DRINSHEAMEC)

10. _____ what you sit on in the mall
(CHENB) to watch people going by

12. _____ phrase describing a mall that
(PONE RIA) is not covered (two words)

13. _____ a small structure or stand
(SKIKO) from which things are sold

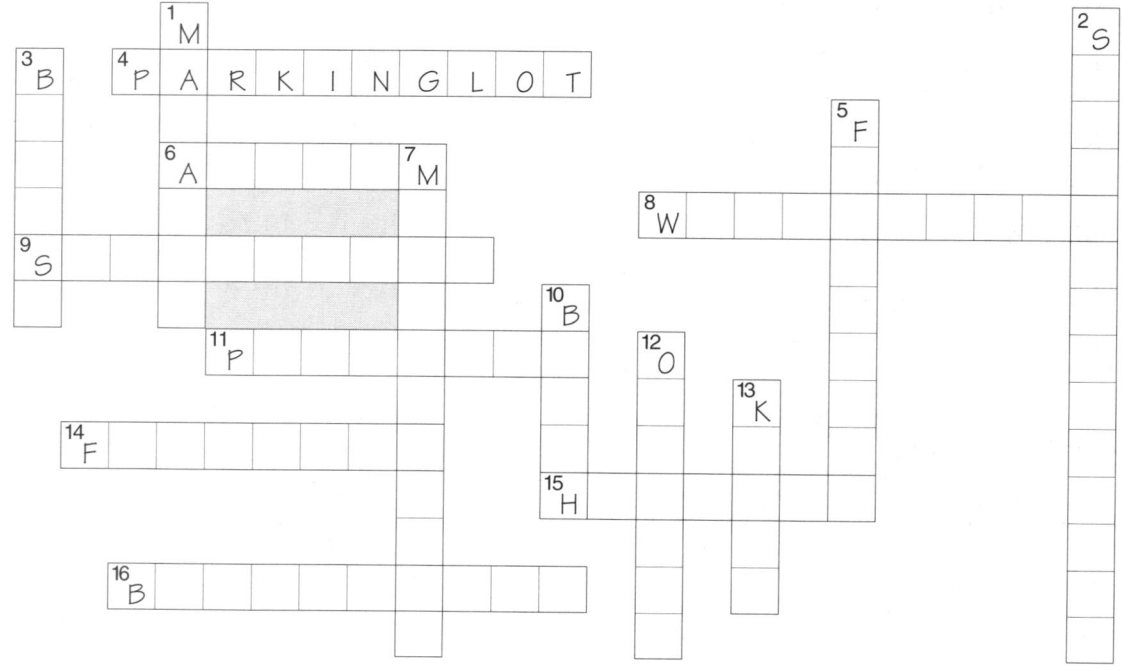

Name: _____ Date: _____

Directions: Complete the sentences with crossword puzzle answers from page 76.

1. Graciela's lovely home has a two-story _____ right in the middle of it.

2. I'm not going to buy anything at the mall today. I just want to _____ with my friends.

3. Let's not go to that store—all of their _____ is old and out-of-date.

4. The _____ at the shoe store was very helpful.

5. My grandmother shouldn't sit on that _____—it's too low for her.

6. If you want to apply for a job, speak to the store _____.

7. I'll meet you at the jewelry _____ in front of the pet shop.

8. If we eat at the _____, we can each get the kind of food we want.

9. When a store employee offers to help me, I say, "No, thanks. I'd just like to _____."

10. While I walk in the mall for exercise, I always _____.

11. We don't have a big mall in our town, but we do have a small _____.

Name: _____ **Date:** _____

It's time to brush up on sports terminology.

Directions: Unscramble the words that match the definitions. Then use the unscrambled words to complete the crossword puzzle. Clue 1-Across has been done for you.

ACROSS

1. _match_ (CHAMT) — a game or contest between two players or teams

3. _____ (MUSITAD) — outdoor sports facility with rows of seats around a large open field

5. _____ (TRAQUER) — one of four equal parts of a game such as football or basketball

6. _____ (LARLY) — a large group of people who have gathered for the same purpose

9. _____ (QUARCET) — a round or oval frame with a network of strings and a handle; used in tennis and other sports (alternate spelling)

12. _____ (DUNWHOTOC) — a six-point score in football

13. _____ (KIRN) — a smooth surface of ice or wood for skating

14. _____ (EPP) — enthusiastic energy

DOWN

2. _____ (TROCU) — a space measured and marked out for playing some game

3. _____ (TSE) — in tennis, a group of six or more games won by a margin of two or more games

4. _____ (TONARMAH) — a footrace of 26 miles, 385 yards

7. _____ (VELO) — in tennis, a score of zero

8. _____ (FLAH-METI) — the rest period between the halves of a game

10. _____ (NINGIN) — one-ninth of a baseball game

11. _____ (COJK) — common nickname for an athlete

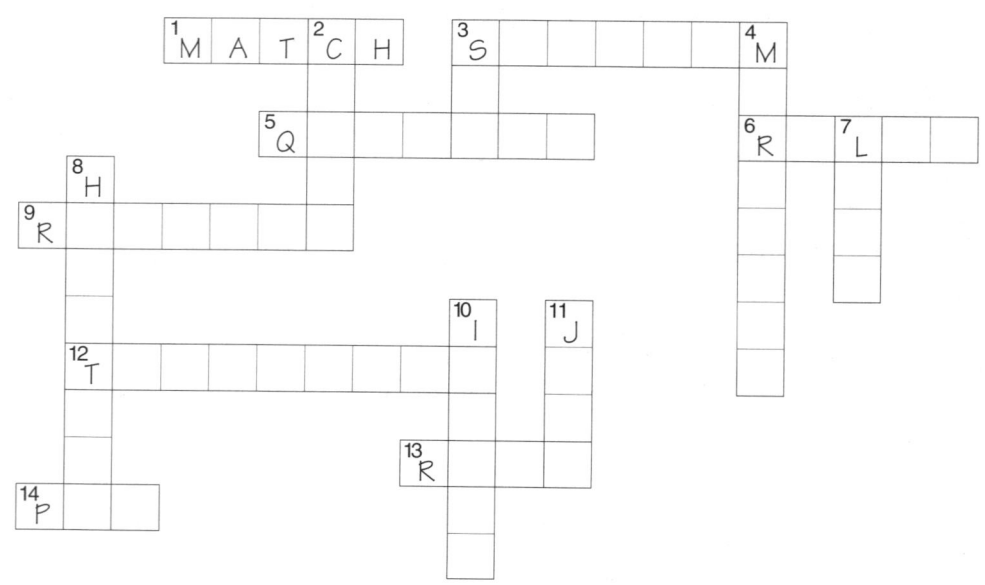

Name: _____   **Date:** _____

Directions: Complete the sentences with crossword puzzle answers from page 78.

1. Many schools have a large

   _____ _____

   before every ball game.

2. Which usually has more runners—
   the Boston or the New York

   _____?

3. Did you know that it is possible to
   win a football game without scoring

   a single _____?

4. The score in this tennis _____ is still _____ all.
   Is anyone ever going to make a point?

5. The _____ show at the Orange Bowl is usually pretty
   amazing.

6. The floor of that old basketball _____ is made of parquet.

7. Every New Year's Day, the Rose Bowl game is played in the same

   _____.

8. The most exciting play in last night's football game was in the fourth

   _____.

9. Tina can't play tennis today—she broke a string on her _____.

10. In professional baseball, there's a tradition of taking a break during the

    seventh _____.

11. Next Halloween we're going to have a costume party at the ice-skating

    _____.

Name: _____   **Date:** _____

Are you well-stocked with "weather words"?

Directions: Unscramble the words that match the definitions. Then use the unscrambled words to complete the crossword puzzle. Clue 10-Down has been done for you.

ACROSS

1. _____ a strong wind with
(DRONWIMTS) little or no rain

3. _____ all the air around
(STOREAMEPH) the earth

6. _____ a very sudden,
(STRUDCULOB) heavy rain

9. _____ any wild storm
(SPETTEM) with high winds
and, often, rain

11. _____ the scientific term
(MUSTINA) for 9-down; a
Japanese word

12. _____ a cyclone that
(THNOOPY) starts over water,
in the warmer
Pacific Ocean

14. _____ a cyclone that
(CRINHUARE) starts over water,
usually in the
West Indies
(Atlantic Ocean)

DOWN

2. _____ another form of a cyclone; a high, narrow
(DROOTAN) column of air over land, whirling very fast,
capable of destroying everything in its path

4. _____ a season when the winds blow from the
(SNOONOM) southwest, bringing daily rain

5. _____ the amount or degree of moisture in the air
(DITHUIMY)

7. _____ the level of heat in the air (or water,
(PRUMTEETARE) or body, etc.)

8. _____ an instrument that measures the pressure
(TROMEBRAE) of the atmosphere

9. _____ a very large, damaging wave, caused by an
(DAILT AVEW) earthquake or very strong wind (2 words)

10. _cyclone_ a storm with very strong winds moving
(LOCCNEY) around a center of low pressure

13. _____ frozen raindrops
(ALIH)

Building Vocabulary Skills and Strategies, Level 6 • Saddleback Publishing, Inc. ©2004 • 3 Watson, Irvine, CA 92618 • Phone (888) SDL-BACK • www.sdlback.com

Name: _____   Date: _____

Directions: Complete the sentences with crossword puzzle answers from page 80.

1. An instrument called a _____ indicates whether or not you can expect good weather.

2. Relative _____ is a comparison of how much moisture is in the air with how much moisture *could* be in the air.

3. Daily thunderstorms are common during the _____ season.

4. In the summer, the _____ in southern Arizona is often higher than 100 degrees.

5. If a 100-foot _____ hit the coast of California, many people could die.

6. William Shakespeare wrote a famous play called *The* _____.

7. Many a _____ has hit the coastline of the southeastern United States.

8. A few years ago, a deadly _____ struck Oklahoma City.

9. As the temperature in rain clouds gets colder, rain can turn into _____.

10. In the spring, a _____ in Texas often kicks up a lot of dust.

11. Tornadoes, hurricanes, and typhoons could alternately be called _____.

Name: _____   **Date:** _____

Music can be instrumental (made by instruments) or vocal (made by singing).

Directions: Unscramble the words that match the definitions. Then use the unscrambled words to complete the crossword puzzle. Clue 1-Down has been done for you.

ACROSS

5. _____ two musicians performing together
   (T U D E)

7. _____ describing musical instruments whose strings vibrate to make music
   (G R E D I N T S)

8. _____ a large group of musicians playing together
   (S C O R T H E R A)

9. _____ musician who performs alone
   (S T I O L O S)

13. _____ describing musical instruments made of brass and having a cup-shaped mouthpiece
    (S A R B S)

14. _____ describing musical instruments that were once made of wood, having a mouthpiece into which the player blows to produce music
    (D I O W N O W D)

15. _____ a person who directs any group of musicians
    (D R U C T O C O N)

16. _____ a small group of musicians playing or singing together
    (S N E B E L E M)

DOWN

1. _musician_ a person skilled in music
   (C I M I S U N A)

2. _____ a musical program, especially one in which a number of musicians perform together
   (T O R C N E C)

3. _____ four musicians performing together
   (T R U A Q E T)

4. _____ a formal presentation before an audience
   (F R E E P R A C M O N)

6. _____ describing instruments that make music by striking or shaking them
   (S C U P O R E N I S)

10. _____ three musicians performing together
    (R O T I)

11. _____ a group of musicians playing different instruments
    (N D A B)

12. _____ the first time a person performs before the public
    (U T B E D)

Name: _____

Date: _____

Directions: Complete the sentences with crossword puzzle answers from page 82.

1. The _____ of our school choir has an excellent reputation.

2. Drums are _____ instruments.

3. Trumpets are _____ instruments.

4. In our _____, I sing alto and she sings soprano.

5. Usually, an _____ plays the music for a ballet.

6. Gregg has not performed publicly before; this is his _____.

7. The senior class gave a _____ of *The Music Man* at the state musical contest.

8. My mom and I are wearing formal dresses to the _____ at Constitution Hall.

9. The clarinet is a _____ instrument.

10. The violin and guitar are _____ instruments.

11. Uncle Jasper and three of his friends sing in a barbershop _____.

Name: _____   **Date:** _____

Monuments are things like statues or buildings that commemorate a person or an event. Some monuments are called *memorials*. Example: The Lincoln Memorial in Washington, D.C., commemorates President Abraham Lincoln.

A. Directions: Write a letter to match each **boldface** monument or memorial with what it commemorates.

1. _____ **George Washington Carver National Monument (Missouri)**

2. _____ **Jefferson Memorial (Washington, D.C.)**

3. _____ **Liberty Bell (Pennsylvania)**

4. _____ **Johnstown Flood National Memorial (Pennsylvania)**

5. _____ **Little Bighorn Battlefield National Monument (Montana)**

6. _____ **Tomb of the Unknown Soldier (Virginia)**

7. _____ **USS Arizona Memorial (Hawaii)**

8. _____ **Wright Brothers National Monument (North Carolina)**

a. the *inventors* of the first airplane to fly successfully

b. the American *scientist* who developed many products from peanuts, soybeans, and other plants

c. the *battle* between General George Custer and Chief Sitting Bull of the Dakota tribe

d. the sinking of this ship during the *bombing* of Pearl Harbor on December 7, 1941

e. the people who died in a great *flood* in 1888

f. all soldiers who died in battle without having been *identified*

g. the author of the *Declaration of Independence* and the third president of the United States

h. the *announcement* of the independence of the United States

B. Directions: Write three original sentences using *italicized* words from Part A.

1. _____

_____

2. _____

_____

3. _____

Name: _____   Date: _____

Some monuments and memorials are also landmarks. But there are many landmarks that are not monuments. Example: the Golden Gate Bridge in California.

A. Directions: Write a letter to match each **boldface** landmark with why it is well-known.

1. _____ **Space Needle (Seattle)**

2. _____ **Empire State Building (New York City)**

3. _____ **Matterhorn (Switzerland)**

4. _____ **Tower of London (England)**

5. _____ **Taj Mahal (India)**

6. _____ **Grand Canyon (Arizona)**

7. _____ **Niagara Falls (between Lake Erie and Lake Ontario)**

8. _____ **Mount Everest (between Tibet and Nepal)**

a. More than a mile deep, it was *carved* out by the Colorado River.

b. the *highest* point on the face of the earth

c. The largest of its kind in North America, it lies between *Canada* and the United States.

d. steep, pyramid-shaped *peak*

e. built for the world's *fair* in 1962

f. Located in *Manhattan*, it was the tallest building in the world for many years.

g. Over the centuries, many *political* prisoners were imprisoned here.

h. A geometrically perfect building in Asia, it was built by a very *wealthy* man for his bride.

B. Directions: Write four original sentences using *italicized* words from Part A.

1. _____

_____

2. _____

_____

3. _____

_____

4. _____

_____

Name: _____   **Date:** _____

In ancient times, people acquired goods and services through trade. Today it's much easier!

A. Directions: Write a letter to match each **boldface** item on the left with its definition on the right. Try guessing first; then check a dictionary to be sure.

1. _____ **yen**

2. _____ **rate of exchange**

3. _____ **drachma**

4. _____ **currency**

5. _____ **peso**

6. _____ **krone**

7. _____ **counterfeit**

8. _____ **won**

9. _____ **pound**

10. _____ **rupee**

a. unit of money in South Korea

b. the money commonly used in a country

c. unit of money in several countries, including Argentina, Colombia, Cuba, and the Philippines

d. unit of money in Greece

e. unit of money in Japan

f. unit of money in Sweden

g. how much one currency is worth in another currency

h. unit of money in India and Pakistan

i. imitation money, intended to cheat people

j. unit of money in several countries, including Great Britain, Ireland, Egypt, and the Sudan

B. Directions: Complete each sentence with a word or phrase from the box. Use each word or phrase only once.

your money's worth	check	savings	teller	credit card

1. At the bank, Trevor waits for the _____ named Susan to help him.

2. Sharon puts 25 percent of each paycheck into a _____ account.

3. If you want to get _____ when you shop, buy items *on sale*.

4. Lance couldn't buy anything because he'd already reached the limit on his _____.

5. Mandy wrote a $20 _____ as a gift for her niece's birthday.

Name: _____   **Date:** _____

A wise man once said, "Earn all you can. Save all you can. Give all you can." Why do you think he didn't include *spending* in that piece of advice?

A. Directions: Use the words and phrases from the box to complete each sentence. Use each word or phrase only once.

bank cards	moneybags (slang)	money belt
money order	on the money (slang)	money-changer

1. After you arrive in Mexico, will you take your dollars to a _____?

2. The _____ issued by Jennifer's bank have the customers' pictures on them.

3. Irene will purchase a _____ to pay for her magazine subscription.

4. Congratulations! Your test answers are right _____!

5. Mr. Jefferson is so rich that his old friends call him "_____."

6. When you're traveling, one of the safest ways to carry money is in a _____.

B. Directions: Write an original sentence using each word or phrase from the box.

credit card	check	savings account	on the money	counterfeit

1. _____

_____

2. _____

_____

3. _____

_____

4. _____

_____

5. _____

_____

Name: _____ **Date:** _____

Do you know these words about different levels and kinds of education?

Directions: Unscramble the words that match the definitions. Then use the unscrambled words to complete the crossword puzzle. Clue 1-Down has been done for you.

ACROSS

4. _____ the subjects of a general college
(BRALLIE RATS) course of study, including literature, languages, history, math, etc. (2 words)

8. _____ a school that usually includes
(DEMILD) grades 6 through 8

10. _____ class that prepares 5-year-olds
(GRANTIKERNDE) for regular schoolwork

11. _____ a degree given to someone who
(STREAM'S) has completed a course of study higher than a bachelor's degree

12. _____ a school of higher education
(TRYUNISEVI) made up of colleges and professional schools

13. _____ a rank awarded by a college to
(GEEDER) a student who has successfully completed a course of study

14. _____ A ____ college usually offers
(TOMICUMYN) a 2-year Associate of Arts degree.

15. _____ a gift of money to
(PALCHISORSH) help a student pay for school costs

DOWN

1. _college___ a school attended after high
(GLOCELE) school to pursue higher studies

2. _____ skilled work done with the hands
(DRETA) that requires special training (such as plumbing); often taught at vocational schools

3. _____ a school that includes grades
(TEENMYLARE) 1 through 5 (and sometimes 6, 7, or 8)

5. _____ money paid by a student to
(INTIUTO) attend a college or private school

6. _____ a certificate that shows that a
(ALDIMOP) student has completed a certain course of study

7. _____ a school that usually includes
(ROJINU GHIH) grades 7, 8, and 9 (2 words)

9. _____ the degree awarded by a college
(CLAROBESH') or university to someone who has completed a four-year course of study

Name: _____   Date: _____

Directions: Complete the sentences with crossword puzzle answers from page 88.

1. Tracy is a third-grader at South Ward _____ School.

2. Before starting _____, Benny went to preschool.

3. Our town doesn't have a junior high school. Students go directly from _____ school to high school.

4. Maria attended the local _____ college before going on to the university.

5. To learn a _____, you should attend a vocational school.

6. After your bachelor's degree, it usually takes about two years to earn a _____ degree.

7. My folks framed my brother's high school _____ and hung it over the fireplace.

8. After four years at Stanford University, I got my bachelor's _____.

9. You might get a _____ to college if your high school grades are good enough.

10. The _____ at private universities is very expensive.

Have you got the vocabulary to deal effectively with injury or illness?

Directions: Unscramble the words that match the definitions. Then use the unscrambled words to complete the crossword puzzle. Clue 1-Across has been done for you.

ACROSS

1. _technician_ (CICHENNITA) someone skilled at such things as drawing blood from a patient

5. _____ (RENUS) a medical professional trained to take care of sick people

11. _____ (CANSHIPIY) another term for *doctor*

12. _____ (BLOYRATORA) a place where medical tests are done in a hospital

13. _____ (STIENVIEN ACRE TUNI) called the ICU, the unit in a hospital that provides special care for seriously ill people (3 words)

14. _____ (DOLOB SERPUSER) vital sign measured by pumping air into a cuff on the arm and slowly releasing the air (2 words)

15. _____ (ESIASED) an illness or sickness

DOWN

2. _____ (GREENCEMY OROM) called the ER, a place where people who urgently need treatment are examined and treated (2 words)

3. _____ (PHITOLAS) a place where doctors, nurses, etc. take care of sick or hurt people over a period of one or more days

4. _____ (LATHEH) freedom from sickness

6. _____ (TOMMYSP) a sign of disease, like a rash; what you complain about to the doctor

7. _____ (BLAMCENUA) a special vehicle for quickly transporting sick or injured people

8. _____ (SLUPE) a regular beating in the arteries, caused by the heart pumping blood

9. _____ (LICCIN) a place where people are examined and treated by a group of doctors

10. _____ (SINOGASID) after a medical examination, the doctor's opinion of what is wrong with the patient

1-Across: T E C H N I C I A N

4 H
5 N
6 S
7 A
8 P
9 C
10 D
11 P
12 L
13 I
14 B
15 D

Name: _____ Date: _____

Directions: Complete the sentences with crossword puzzle answers from page 90.

1. Dr. Ullman is the _____ I see on a regular basis.

2. The Downtown _____ has four doctors. You don't have to wait long to see a doctor there.

3. Nowadays, it is common for a man to become a _____. In the 20th century, that job was done mostly by women.

4. It is unusual to find a full-service _____ in a small town.

5. As the _____ sped by, I saw the flashing lights and heard the siren.

6. In an _____, it's not "first come, first served." The most serious cases are treated first.

7. I discovered that my cough was a _____ of pneumonia.

8. Uncle Zeke was surprised by the doctor's _____. He was allergic to dogs!

9. The _____ who drew blood from my arm was very skilled. It didn't hurt at all.

10. A technician examined my blood sample at the hospital's _____.

11. Good _____ is one of the most valuable things in the world.

HOSPITAL

EMERGENCY

AMBULANCE

SCREECH!

To *invent* is to think out or make something that didn't exist before.

A. Directions: Write a letter to match each **boldface** inventor with his invention.

1. _____ **Samuel B. Morse**
2. _____ **Alexander Graham Bell**
3. _____ **George Washington Carver**
4. _____ **Thomas Edison**
5. _____ **Albert Einstein**
6. _____ **Henry Shrapnel**
7. _____ **King Camp Gillette**
8. _____ **Louis Braille**
9. _____ **Louis Pasteur**
10. _____ **Eli Whitney**
11. _____ **Daniel Fahrenheit**
12. _____ **George Ferris**
13. _____ **Johann Gutenberg**
14. _____ **George Pullman**

a. the cotton gin

b. the light bulb, the *microphone*, motion pictures

c. the Ferris wheel

d. the *theory* of relativity

e. alcohol and mercury thermometers

f. the safety razor

g. a type of *artillery* shell

h. the printing press

i. railroad cars with sleeping *berths*

j. 450 products made from peanuts and other plants

k. the telephone

l. the telegraph code

m. a system of printing and writing for the blind

n. the process of *pasteurization*

B. Directions: Write five original sentences using the *italicized* words from Part A. Check a dictionary if you need help with word meaning.

1. _____
   _____
2. _____
   _____
3. _____
   _____
4. _____
   _____
5. _____
   _____

Name: _____   **Date:** _____

If you *discover* something, you are the *first* to find or learn it.

Directions: Complete the sentences with words or phrases from the box.

Pacific Ocean	trade route	the Hawaiian Islands	radium	penicillin
North Pole	Halley's Comet	Cape of Good Hope	South Pole	"new world"

1. In 1911, many explorers contributed to the discovery of the _____. But the Antarctic explorer who arrived there first was Roald Amundsen, a Norwegian.

2. The discovery of _____ by Marie and Pierre Curie made certain cancer treatments possible.

3. Alexander Fleming discovered _____, an extremely important antibiotic.

4. Robert Peary received most of the credit for discovering the _____. What is not so well-known is that his co-discoverer was Matthew Henson, an African-American.

5. In 1803, President Thomas Jefferson hired the explorers Meriwether Lewis and William Clark. Their job was to follow the Missouri and Columbia Rivers and find an overland route to the _____.

6. Christopher Columbus gets most of the credit for discovering the _____. Of course, the Native Americans lived there first! And not only did Leif Erikson explore the North American mainland as early as the year 1000, but Viking maps of northeast Canada dated around the year 1440 have been found.

7. Edmond Halley did not discover _____, but he was the first to successfully predict when it would reappear.

8. In the 8th century, Polynesians discovered and colonized _____.

9. Marco Polo established the first overland _____ between Europe and China.

10. Vasco da Gama discovered a route to India by way of the _____ (at the southern tip of Africa).

Name: _____   **Date:** _____

Let's "work" with some words that you will encounter in the working world.

Directions: Unscramble the words that match the definitions. Then use the unscrambled words to complete the crossword puzzle. Clue 2-Across has been done for you.

ACROSS

2. _interview_ (TRIWENVIE) a meeting between people to share information

5. _____ (TANDECADI) a person who seeks or has been recommended for a job (or a political office)

8. _____ (PRIVOUSSER) a person who directs or manages a group of workers

9. _____ (SLOONECUR) a person whose job it is to advise others

11. _____ (ENCRES) to test and question people in order to separate them into groups

12. _____ (AIRNEET) a person being trained in something

13. _____ (PUTTADIE) a natural ability or talent

14. _____ (KICS AVEEL) paid time off for illness or injury (2 words)

DOWN

1. _____ (MUNAH SCEERUROS) called the HR department, it creates new job openings, manages employee benefits, and may train new employees (2 words)

3. _____ (MENTRIERET) state of having given up your work, usually because of age

4. _____ (SWEAG) money paid to workers according to the amount of work done

6. _____ (NANULA AVEEL) paid vacation time (2 words)

7. _____ (SMURÉÉ) a prepared record of your work experience and education; used for job-hunting purposes

8. _____ (ALSYRA) a fixed amount of money paid to workers at regular times

10. _____ (TRENNI) a person who is learning by working with people already trained in that field; often a temporary job

Crossword grid:

2 Across (row): I N T E R V I E W

Grid letters shown:
- 1 Down: H
- 4 Down: W
- 5 Across: C
- 6 Down: A
- 7 Down: R
- 8 Across/Down: S
- 9 Across: C
- 10 Down: I
- 11 Across: S
- 12 Across: T
- 13 Across: A
- 14 Across: S

Name: _____   **Date:** _____

Directions: Complete the sentences with crossword puzzle answers from page 94.
Hint: In these sentences, some of the answers are used as *plurals*.

1. An attractive, well-prepared _____ may be your first contact with an employer. Make it a good one!

2. Before you _____ with someone for a new job, prepare yourself. Practice with a friend.

3. If a company likes your résumé, someone in its _____ _____ department will probably contact you.

4. Try to get a summer job as an _____. If the employer likes your work, you may be hired again later.

5. It's a good idea to use your _____ from work only when it's really necessary.

6. Most employers give employees about 10 days of _____ every year. You can use those days a few at a time, or all at once.

7. A _____ stands between employees and higher-level managers.

8. Career _____ often work in high schools and colleges. They can help you decide what occupation may match your skills.

9. An _____ test can reveal your natural talents.

10. There may be many _____ competing for the job you're seeking.

11. The HR department usually _____ all incoming résumés before passing the best ones on to management.

Name: _____   **Date:** _____

Ready to hit the road? Here are some words that will help you behind the wheel.

Directions: Unscramble the words that match the definitions. Then use the unscrambled words to complete the crossword puzzle. Clue 5-Across has been done for you.

ACROSS

5. _drive_ (VERDI) to control the movement of a vehicle

7. _____ (TREBNOCLIVE) an automobile with a top that can be folded back

8. _____ (LUNAMA) done with the hands

10. _____ (SMINRIOSTANS) the part of a car that sends power from the engine to the wheels

11. _____ (CATATOMUI) working by itself, on its own

13. _____ (ELANEDUD) without lead in it; the kind of gasoline that's better for the environment

14. _____ (REWOP) force or energy from electricity, gasoline, etc.

DOWN

1. _____ (TENOCA) the substance in gasoline that helps prevent engine "knocking"

2. _____ (SKEARB) the devices used to slow down or stop a vehicle

3. _____ (TREGINES) controlling a vehicle by means of a wheel

4. _____ (WELDISAL) the part of a tire between the wheel and the tread

6. _____ (VIMANIN) a small version of a closed panel truck; used for carrying passengers

7. _____ (SCICALS) of lasting quality and popularity

9. _____ (CUPPIK) a small, open truck used for hauling light loads

12. _____ (AKME) the brand of a motor vehicle

Directions: Complete the sentences with crossword puzzle answers from page 96.
Hint: In these sentences, some of the answers are used as *plurals*.

1. Larry's dad has a beautiful

   _____ car

   that was built in 1924.

2. You have to be careful when

   you drive a car with power

   _____ for

   the first time. If you push too

   hard, you might throw your

   passenger against the windshield.

3. A _____ may

   be a good choice for a family with

   lots of kids.

4. Most rental cars take only _____ gas.

5. Giorgio's car has an _____, rather than a manual,

   transmission. It has four forward gears.

6. Cars that have power _____ are great for people who

   have weak or injured arms.

7. When I moved to Dalhart, Texas, I saw more _____

   trucks than I ever saw in California.

8. On a sunny day it's great fun to drive a _____ with

   the top down.

9. Tires with white _____ used to be very popular.

10. Does your family always buy the same _____ of car?

11. High-_____ gasoline is the most expensive.

Name: _____ **Date:** _____

The word *strike* can be used in many ways. Some of this word's meanings are informal or slang. All are in the dictionary.

A. Directions: Read the three definitions under each **boldface** expression. Then circle the correct definition.

1. to **go on strike**

   go on a hitting binge

   stop work as a protest

   march in a band

2. to be **struck dumb**

   become speechless

   be hit very hard

   make a stupid remark

3. to **strike home**

   hit your house

   have a desired effect

   stop doing housework

4. to **strike it rich**

   suddenly become wealthy

   use expensive matches

   get lots of hits in baseball

5. to **strike something off**

   throw it away

   brush something off of you

   cross out something on a list

6. to **strike out**

   get three strikes in baseball

   hit a home run

   stop working hard

7. to **strike up**

   start something

   make someone angry

   batter up in baseball

8. to **strike a coin**

   toss a coin

   make a coin

   give a coin away

9. to **strike a campsite**

   vandalize a camp

   take down or take apart a camp

   rob or steal from a camp

B. Directions: Write original sentences using any three of the **boldface** expressions above.

1. _____

   _____

2. _____

   _____

3. _____

   _____

Name: _____ **Date:** _____

Aha! Here are some more interesting expressions—this time the main word is *throw*.

A. **Directions:** Read the three definitions under each **boldface** expression. Then circle the correct definition.

1. to **throw someone for a loop**

    toss someone over your head

    swing someone in a circle

    badly confuse someone

2. to **throw** a contest

    deliberately lose

    judge unfairly

    vigorously participate

3. to **throw up**

    cheat   vomit

        give up

4. to **throw in the towel**

    give up

    launder the towel

    become allies with someone

5. to **throw off** a cold

    give it to someone

    get rid of it

    warm up a room

6. to **throw together**

    quickly prepare something

    glue two things together

    think like someone else

7. to **throw a fit**

    exercise your arms

    misbehave out of anger

    host a barbecue

8. to be a **throwback**

    a type of football player

    a skillful catcher

    like a primitive type

9. to **throw a switch**

    cut the wires

    turn it on or off

    exchange places

B. **Directions:** Write original sentences using any three of the **boldface** expressions above.

1. _____

    _____

2. _____

    _____

3. _____

    _____

Name: _____   **Date:** _____

The *histories*, or origins, of many words can be traced to other languages or earlier versions of English.

---

aggravate   from a Latin word meaning "to make heavier"

quash   from a Latin word meaning "to shatter" or "to shake"

yolk   from Old English, meaning "the yellow part"

dreary   in Old English, it meant "bloody" or "gory"

venal   from a Latin word meaning "for sale"

rival   from a Latin word meaning "a person who lives near or uses the same stream as another person"

shenanigans   thought to be from an Irish word meaning, "I play the fox" (the fox being a tricky, sly animal)

caterpillar   from the Latin words *catta*, meaning "a cat," and *pilosus*, meaning "hair"

Directions: Use the **boldface** words in the box to complete the sentences. If necessary, reread the word origins to help you figure out the answers. Check the dictionary if you're not sure.

1. A _____ politician is one who accepts money in exchange for illegal favors.

2. A dictator will always try to _____ a rebellion, usually with force.

3. My twin brothers are up to their usual _____. This time they'll be grounded for a week!

4. If you go out jogging, you may _____ your sore leg.

5. A _____ is the larva of a butterfly.

6. Does Janine's boyfriend have a new _____ for her affections?

7. If you like sunshine, you may think that Seattle's climate is too _____ and depressing.

8. If you're frying an egg for me, I like the _____ runny and the white solid.

Name: _____   **Date:** _____

Directions: Write original sentences using the **boldface** words.

1. **aggravate** _____

_____

_____

_____

2. **quash** _____

_____

_____

_____

3. **yolk** _____

_____

4. **dreary** _____

_____

5. **rival** _____

_____

6. **shenanigans** _____

_____

7. **caterpillar** _____

_____

8. **venal** _____

_____

Name: _____   **Date:** _____

All the sentences in a paragraph deal with a particular point—the *topic* of the paragraph. Did you know that sentences can have topics, too?

Directions: Write a letter to match each **boldface** topic with the sentence it describes. The first one has been done for you.

1. _e_ **research**

2. ____ **spiritualism**

3. ____ **gluttony**

4. ____ **commitment**

5. ____ **anxiety**

6. ____ **preservation**

7. ____ **digestion**

8. ____ **rumors**

9. ____ **intolerance**

10. ____ **faith**

11. ____ **bowling**

12. ____ **materialism**

a. My parents believe in me, and I know they will never let me down.

b. According to Garry, Jen and Walt are breaking up. Sherry says that Jen doesn't want to.

c. While Sid usually scores about 250, I can't even keep the ball out of the gutter!

d. Heartburn can be caused by eating too many fats.

e. Scientists all over the world are trying to find a cure for cancer.

f. The Jets dislike the Sharks because their nationalities are different.

g. All our club members ever think about is money and clothes!

h. Ursula believes that her aunt can communicate with ghosts.

i. Protecting our national monuments from decay is an important job.

j. Real worriers can agonize over anything, no matter how unimportant.

k. Brandy's whole family eats more than they need to.

l. Val's problem is that she cannot maintain a relationship for very long.

Name: _____

Date: _____

A. **Directions:** Write an original sentence about each **boldface** topic. Try to use synonyms for the topic words. Use a dictionary or thesaurus if you need help.

1. **spiritualism** _____

   _____

2. **gluttony** _____

   _____

3. **commitment** _____

   _____

4. **anxiety** _____

   _____

5. **preservation** _____

   _____

6. **digestion** _____

   _____

7. **rumors** _____

   _____

8. **intolerance** _____

   _____

9. **faith** _____

   _____

10. **materialism** _____

   _____

B. **Directions:** Now write two topic words of your own. Then write a sentence that illustrates each topic.

1. _____ _____

   _____

2. _____ _____

   _____

Name: _____ **Date:** _____

Alligators, bears, and *cheetahs!* Here are some more ABC words that you should know.

Directions: Use context clues to help you complete each sentence with the correct **boldface** word. Use each word only once.

advocate	**bedrock**	**carpenter**
almanac	**blemish**	**chimpanzee**
aquarium	**boast**	**conclusive**
astonish	**bunkhouse**	**crease**

1. If the _____ is too close to the surface, we can't build a house with a basement.

2. Experience has proven that an adult _____ does not make a good pet.

3. I _____ my folks every time I bring home an A in math!

4. LaNell irons a _____ in her blue jeans before wearing them.

5. Every time my sister gets a _____, she puts a bandage on it!

6. Brett is in some trouble. He needs an _____ to present his side of the story to the Student Council.

7. If I'd just flunked history for the second time, I surely wouldn't _____ about it!

8. My favorite _____ has a terrific squid tank!

9. If you like working with wood, you might consider becoming a _____.

10. The results of the survey weren't _____. They don't prove anything.

11. At camp, I was the senior group leader for _____ No. 7.

12. Farmers once used the _____ to guide them in planting their crops.

Name: _____   **Date:** _____

A. **Directions:** Use each **boldface** word in an original sentence.

1. **advocate** _____

_____

2. **aquarium** _____

_____

3. **astonish** _____

_____

4. **blemish** _____

_____

5. **boast** _____

_____

6. **bunkhouse** _____

_____

7. **carpenter** _____

_____

8. **chimpanzee** _____

_____

9. **conclusive** _____

_____

10. **crease** _____

_____

B. **Directions:** Now write ABC words of your own and tell what each word means. If you're not sure, check a dictionary.

A word: _____   _____

B word: _____   _____

C word: _____   _____

Name: _____   **Date:** _____

Dogs, eels, and frogs*! Have fun with these DEF words!*

Directions: Complete the sentences with the **boldface** words. Use each word only once.

dainty	eavesdrop	faulty
deadlocked	elegy	fervent
diligent	embassy	flatter
douse	excavate	fragile

1. The poet wrote an _____ to commemorate the fallen war hero.

2. After the flood, the Red Cross made a _____ appeal for help.

3. My project team in biology class is extremely _____. We'll finish before everyone else.

4. Have you ever visited a foreign _____? Many of them are located in Washington, D.C.

5. Can we talk in person? If we talk on the phone, my little brother will _____.

6. It is dangerous to _____ an electrical fire with water.

7. A mining company recently started to _____ that old silver mine.

8. Be sure you mark the package "_____." We don't want anything to get broken.

9. The car won't start. One of the spark plugs must be _____.

10. No one is ever going to describe a six-footer as _____.

11. You _____ me, Eldon. I'm not gorgeous—just beautiful.

12. The baseball game has gone into the 13th inning. The teams are really _____.

A. Directions: Use each **boldface** word in an original sentence.

1. **dainty** _____

_____

2. **deadlocked** _____

_____

3. **diligent** _____

_____

4. **douse** _____

_____

5. **eavesdrop** _____

_____

6. **embassy** _____

_____

7. **excavate** _____

_____

8. **faulty** _____

_____

9. **flatter** _____

_____

10. **fragile** _____

_____

B. Directions: Now write three DEF words of your own and explain what each word means. Check a dictionary if you're not sure.

D word: _____ _____

E word: _____ _____

F word: _____ _____

Name: _____ **Date:** _____

Gnus, hyenas, and *iguanas!* More alphabet words—this time, GHI!

Directions: Complete the sentences with the **boldface** words. Use each word only once.

gall	hacker	illegible
gimmick	heliport	impersonal
goad	horizon	indistinct
grasp	hypocrite	itinerant

1. I can't quite _____ what you're trying to tell me.

2. A _____ is never as honest and loyal as he pretends to be.

3. They claim that their new computer system is fully protected from any _____.

4. _____ preachers usually stay at the same church for only a few years.

5. Pete's got a lot of _____ to be accusing you of cheating on the exam!

6. In the courtroom, most judges behave in an _____ manner.

7. My favorite time of day is just before the sun disappears over the _____.

8. I tried to listen, but their voices were _____ and muffled.

9. It is not true that *all* doctors' handwriting is _____.

10. Is there a _____ on the roof of that tall office building?

11. Lillian has invented the most remarkable _____ for braiding hair!

12. I wish you wouldn't _____ me into dieting. I'll do it when I'm ready.

Name: _____   **Date:** _____

A. **Directions:** Use each **boldface** word in an original sentence.

1. **gall** _____

_____

2. **goad** _____

_____

3. **hacker** _____

_____

4. **heliport** _____

_____

5. **horizon** _____

_____

6. **hypocrite** _____

_____

7. **illegible** _____

_____

8. **impersonal** _____

_____

9. **indistinct** _____

_____

10. **itinerant** _____

_____

B. **Directions:** Now write three GHI words of your own and explain the meaning of each word. If you're not sure, check a dictionary.

G word: _____ _____

H word: _____ _____

I word: _____ _____

Name: _____ **Date:** _____

Jackals, koalas, and *loons!* Here are some new JKL words for you to learn!

Directions: Complete the sentences with the **boldface** words. Use each word only once.

jabber	karate	labyrinth
jealous	kennel	leeway
jeopardy	killjoy	literal
judgment	knoll	lozenge

1. Hallie recently earned her brown belt in _____.

2. The Pentagon often seems like a _____.

3. From the top of that little _____, you can see for miles around.

4. Kids sometimes think their parents drone on and on, and sometimes parents think their kids tend to _____.

5. My throat is very dry. Do you happen to have a _____?

6. In your budget, you have allowed very little _____ for unexpected expenses.

7. People who use drugs put themselves in grave _____.

8. The _____ translation of an English poem into Spanish doesn't sound poetic.

9. I hate to be a _____, but somebody has to remind the kids of their eleven o'clock curfew.

10. Sandra's boyfriend is glad that she isn't a _____ person by nature.

11. When we take car trips, our dog travels in a portable _____.

12. The defendant's guilt or innocence is up to the jury's _____.

Name: _____

Date: _____

A. **Directions:** Use each **boldface** word in an original sentence.

1. **jabber** _____

_____

2. **jealous** _____

_____

3. **jeopardy** _____

_____

4. **judgment** _____

_____

5. **karate** _____

_____

6. **kennel** _____

_____

7. **killjoy** _____

_____

8. **leeway** _____

_____

9. **literal** _____

_____

10. **lozenge** _____

_____

B. **Directions:** Now write three JKL words of your own and explain what each word means. Check a dictionary if you're not sure.

J word: _____ _____

K word: _____ _____

L word: _____ _____

Name: _____   **Date:** _____

Mammoths, narwhals, and octopi! Wow! Lucky for you, the MNO words below are not so exotic.

Directions: Complete the sentences with the **boldface** words. Use each word only once.

makeshift	**name-dropper**	**oath**
megaphone	**nincompoop**	**ointment**
mischievous	**nostalgia**	**ostracize**
muscle	**nutrition**	**overwrought**

1. Years ago, people thought that applying _____ was a good way to treat a burn.

2. Your behavior is outrageous! Sometimes you can be such a _____!

3. Sean is always talking about the important people his father knows. He's such a _____!

4. When we were kids, sometimes we built _____ forts out of packing crates.

5. Deirdre was _____ after nearly being run down in the crosswalk.

6. Some people may _____ Tim if he takes an extreme stand on that issue.

7. When Trudy joined the Air Force, she took an _____ to support the U.S. government.

8. Good _____ requires eating food from all the food groups.

9. The cheerleader used a _____ to make sure the crowd could hear him.

10. Class reunions are full of _____, as old friends remember good times.

11. Both brain power and _____ power contribute to success in sports.

12. The boy didn't mean to do any real harm. He was just being _____.

Name: _____   **Date:** _____

A. Directions: Use each **boldface** word in an original sentence.

1. **makeshift** _____
   _____

2. **mischievous** _____
   _____

3. **muscle** _____
   _____

4. **nincompoop** _____
   _____

5. **nostalgia** _____
   _____

6. **nutrition** _____
   _____

7. **oath** _____
   _____

8. **ointment** _____
   _____

9. **ostracize** _____
   _____

10. **overwrought** _____
    _____

B. Directions: Now write three MNO words of your own and explain each word's meaning. Check a dictionary if you're not sure.

M word: _____ _____

N word: _____ _____

O word: _____ _____

Name: _____   **Date:** _____

Peacocks, quail, and *reindeer!* More animals and more words—P, Q, and R.

Directions: Use the **boldface** words to complete the sentences. Use each word only once.

panhandle	**quadrant**	**ransom**
pedal	**quartz**	**rebound**
plumage	**quibble**	**routine**
preliminary	**quilt**	**ruddy**

1. Tonight's _____ chess match will determine who goes on to the semifinals.

2. My dad's _____ face shows that he just came in from the cold.

3. Georgetown University is in the northwest _____ of Washington, D.C.

4. My best friend sent me a lovely handmade _____ from North Carolina.

5. Some compassionate school children collected money to _____ slaves in Africa.

6. When Nick began dating Priscilla, he was on the _____ from breaking up with Pam.

7. "Put the _____ to the metal" means to hurry up.

8. Why _____ about such an unimportant thing as where to go for dinner?

9. Vanna's beautiful necklace is made of _____ crystal.

10. Which _____ do you think is prettier, a peacock's or a parrot's?

11. My grandma lives in a little town on the Oklahoma _____.

12. After summer vacation, Judi had some difficulty getting back into a regular _____ at school.

Name: _____   **Date:** _____

A. Directions: Use each **boldface** word in an original sentence.

1. **pedal** _____

_____

2. **plumage** _____

_____

3. **preliminary** _____

_____

4. **quadrant** _____

_____

5. **quartz** _____

_____

6. **quibble** _____

_____

7. **quilt** _____

_____

8. **rebound** _____

_____

9. **routine** _____

_____

10. **ruddy** _____

_____

B. Directions: Now write three PQR words of your own and explain what each word means.

P word: _____   _____

Q word: _____   _____

R word: _____   _____

Name: _____   **Date:** _____

Sand dabs and tortoises! Here are some very useful words beginning with *S* and *T*.

Directions: Use the **boldface** words to complete the sentences. Use each word only once.

serene	**shawl**	**smorgasbord**	**tambourine**	**thin-skinned**	**transcribe**
sham	**singe**	**squall**	**telethon**	**thwart**	**tumble**

1. Learning to play a _____ is not very difficult.

2. Randy ate too much at the _____ restaurant.

3. That student's autobiography is a _____. He isn't really related to the Queen of England!

4. The police were able to _____ an attempted robbery at Mrs. McHugh's house.

5. One Christmas, my aunt crocheted a wool _____ for every female in the family.

6. It is not always easy to _____ a doctor's notes on a patient's chart.

7. _____ people take criticism too personally.

8. Jack took a nasty _____ down a flight of cement stairs.

9. Don't go out in the sailboat. I hear there's a _____ underway.

10. Every Labor Day, there's a huge _____ to benefit victims of muscular dystrophy.

11. A quiet pond, surrounded by green grass and willow trees, is a _____ setting for a picnic.

12. Marilyn learned something the hard way: You can _____ your eyelashes and eyebrows when you open a hot oven.

Name: _____   **Date:** _____

A. Directions: Use each **boldface** word in an original sentence.

1. **serene** _____

_____

2. **sham** _____

_____

3. **shawl** _____

_____

4. **singe** _____

_____

5. **smorgasbord** _____

_____

6. **tambourine** _____

_____

7. **thin-skinned** _____

_____

8. **thwart** _____

_____

9. **transcribe** _____

_____

10. **tumble** _____

_____

B. Directions: Now write two S words and two T words of your own. Explain what each word means.

S word: _____ _____

S word: _____ _____

T word: _____ _____

T word: _____ _____

Name: _____   **Date:** _____

Unicorns and *vipers*! Now we're up to *U* and *V*!

Directions: Use the **boldface** words to complete the sentences. Use each word only once.

ultimatum	**unearth**	**upholstery**	**vacant**	**valiant**	**vindictive**
unbiased	**unsightly**	**utopia**	**vacillate**	**ventilate**	**vouch**

1. A good reporter can _____ the hidden facts behind a story.

2. When Kim pulls into the parking lot, Tim looks for a _____ parking space.

3. You don't want to make an enemy of Jill. Sometimes she can be really _____.

4. Don's bedroom is worse than _____; it's a total mess.

5. Mom opens the windows at night to _____ our bedrooms.

6. I'm giving you an _____: Either pay me for the radio or give it back now.

7. The _____ on our old sofa and chairs needs to be replaced.

8. Dina can _____ between two desserts on a menu for ten minutes!

9. You won't hurt my feelings. Tell me the truth. I need your _____ opinion.

10. Freda made a _____ effort to get a good grade in English.

11. I need a character reference for a job application. Will you _____ for me?

12. Unfortunately, there's no perfect place such as a _____. We only *wish* there were.

Name: _____ **Date:** _____

A. **Directions:** Use each **boldface** word in an original sentence.

1. **ultimatum** _____

_____

2. **unbiased** _____

_____

3. **unearth** _____

_____

4. **unsightly** _____

_____

5. **vacant** _____

_____

6. **vacillate** _____

_____

7. **valiant** _____

_____

8. **ventilate** _____

_____

9. **vindictive** _____

_____

10. **vouch** _____

_____

B. **Directions:** Now write two U words and two V words of your own. Explain the meaning of each word.

U word: _____ _____

U word: _____ _____

V word: _____ _____

V word: _____ _____

Name: _____ **Date:** _____

Wallabies, xiphosurans, yaks, and zebras! W, X, Y, Z and the end of the alphabet!

Directions: Use the **boldface** words to complete the sentences. Use each word only once.

wary	**xenon**	**yacht**	**zealous**
weary	**X-ray**	**yearn**	**zoology**
wound	**xylophone**	**yuletide**	**zucchini**

1. My family's favorite vegetable is the _____ squash we grow in our garden.

2. Letty's _____ was deep enough to require stitches.

3. The _____ season causes some people a great deal of stress.

4. I'm so _____ that my muscles are going on strike!

5. If you like animals, _____ may be a good course of study for you.

6. Su Lin is _____ in his pursuit of a gold medal in swimming.

7. Nana may have pneumonia. She may have to get a chest _____ to be sure.

8. Do you often _____ for the good old days? Buy our CD of the best songs of the '70s.

9. _____ is an odorless, colorless gas that's used in lasers.

10. The comedian said that a _____ is just a fancy rowboat with indoor plumbing.

11. My parents don't trust that man. They told us to be _____ of him.

12. You strike wooden or metal bars with a hammer when you play a _____.

Name: _____   **Date:** _____

A. Directions: Use each **boldface** word in an original sentence.

1. **wary** _____

_____

2. **weary** _____

_____

3. **wound** _____

_____

4. **X-ray** _____

_____

5. **xylophone** _____

_____

6. **yacht** _____

_____

7. **yearn** _____

_____

8. **yuletide** _____

_____

9. **zealous** _____

_____

10. **zoology** _____

_____

B. Directions: Now write four WXYZ words of your own and explain what each word means.

W word: _____ _____

X word: _____ _____

Y word: _____ _____

Z word: _____ _____

Name: _____   **Date:** _____

Are you ready for some A to Z word challenges? Use your imagination, and check a dictionary to be sure of word meanings.

Directions: Write a sentence using *either* word given for each letter.

1. **A – audacity, affable** _____

_____

2. **B – banal, balky** _____

_____

3. **C – cannibal, callous** _____

_____

4. **D – dauntless, dynamo** _____

_____

5. **E – eccentric, epitome** _____

_____

6. **F – flamboyant, formidable** _____

_____

7. **G – gossamer, gaunt** _____

_____

8. **H – hapless, habitat** _____

_____

9. **I – ignoramus, implicit** _____

_____

10. **J – jaunty, jovial** _____

_____

11. **K – khaki, kindred** _____

_____

12. **L – laggard, lament** _____

_____

Name: _____ **Date:** _____

Directions: Now write a sentence using *both* words given for each letter. Check a dictionary to be sure of word meanings.

1. **M – manic maestro** _____
   _____
   _____
   _____

2. **N – nocturnal nemesis** _____
   _____

3. **O – obnoxious oboist** _____
   _____

4. **P – persistent peddler** _____
   _____

5. **Q – quaint quotation** _____
   _____

6. **R – rakish rascal** _____
   _____

7. **S – sassy servant** _____
   _____

8. **T – tempestuous teacher** _____
   _____

9. **U – uncouth unicorn** _____
   _____

10. **V – velour valise** _____
    _____

11. **W – wayward whippet** _____
    _____

12. **X, Y – xanthous yam** _____
    _____

13. **Z – zany zombie** _____
    _____

Name: _____   **Date:** _____

Every one of us is a unique person with a unique set of characteristics. What words would you use to describe yourself?

A. **Directions:** From each group of **boldface** words, choose one word that describes *you*. Then use that word in an original sentence about yourself. For example, if you think you are *athletic*, you might write: *Because I am an athletic person, I participate in many different sports.*

1. **garrulous**
   reticent
   assertive

2. **studious**
   carefree
   meticulous

3. **pragmatic**
   idealistic
   realistic

4. **generous**
   thoughtful
   perceptive

5. **steady**
   serious
   humorous

1. _____
   _____
   _____

2. _____
   _____
   _____

3. _____
   _____
   _____

4. _____
   _____
   _____

5. _____
   _____
   _____

B. **Directions:** Choose three words from Part A that do *not* describe you. Use each word in a sentence, explaining why it does not apply to you.

1. _____
   _____

2. _____
   _____

3. _____
   _____

Name: _____   **Date:** _____

"Your world" consists of your home, family, school, friends, community and country—as you see them. Now choose some words to describe your world.

A. Directions: From each group of **boldface** words, choose one word that describes *your* world. Then use that word in an original sentence about your world.

For example, if your community is in the West, you might write: *In my town, we like Western music, Western movies, and Western clothes.*

1. COMMUNITY	2. COMMUNITY	3. TEENAGERS	4. SCHOOL	5. HOME
bucolic	political	trendy	disciplined	apartment
urban	apathetic	conventional	academic	duplex
multicultural	welcoming	cliquey	undemanding	farmhouse
insular	reserved	rowdy	unmanageable	house

1. _____

_____

2. _____

_____

3. _____

_____

4. _____

_____

5. _____

_____

B. Directions: Now choose three words from Part A that do *not* describe your world. Use each word in a sentence, explaining how your world is different.

1. _____

_____

2. _____

_____

3. _____

_____

Name: _____ **Date:** _____

Some activities, such as swimming and horseback riding, involve lots of action. Others, like studying and playing checkers, are much less physical.

A. Directions: Decide whether each **boldface** activity in the box is action-filled or sedentary. Then write the activity in the appropriate column. (Hint: There are eight activities of each kind.)

scull	mahjong
polo	orating
rodeo	patching
combat	calisthenics
darning	cribbage
editing	stampede
fencing	daydreaming
basking	waterskiing

MORE PHYSICAL

_____
_____
_____
_____
_____
_____
_____
_____

LESS PHYSICAL

_____
_____
_____
_____
_____
_____
_____
_____

B. Directions: Solve the crossword puzzle. The clues are definitions of some words from Part A.

ACROSS

3. battle

7. a game from China, played with many small tiles

8. a competition featuring horses, cattle, and cowboys and cowgirls

DOWN

1. a light, narrow racing boat

2. a sudden onrush of many animals or people

4. warming yourself pleasantly

5. a card game; the score is kept with pegs on a small board

6. a game played on horseback

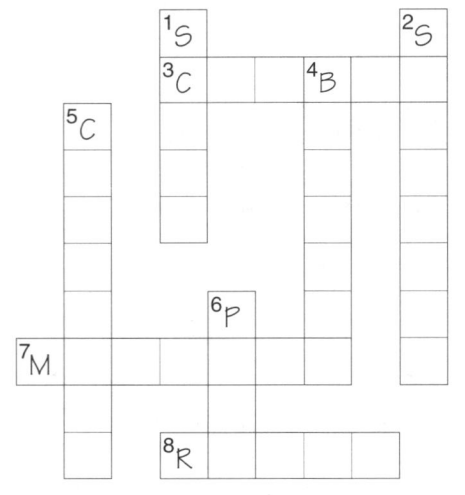

Name: _____   Date: _____

Some activities are both physical and mental.
Others, like *wondering*, are *only* mental.

A. **Directions:** Circle 15 words in the list below that are *mental* activities.

brood	envision	reflect	visualize
ponder	scrutinize	abdicate	deliberate
ferment	suffocate	fantasize	ruminate
recollect	vaccinate	imagine	meditate
perforate	consider	reminisce	contemplate

B. **Directions:** Choose five mental activities from Part A and write an original sentence about each one.

1. _____

_____

2. _____

_____

3. _____

_____

4. _____

_____

5. _____

_____

Name: _____   **Date:** _____

> What do you see when you observe your environment? Look for people and things you never noticed before. When you *really* pay attention, what do you see?

A. **Directions:** Try to look beyond "your world." Then write original sentences describing things (sounds, smells, weather, etc.) or people you never noticed before.

1. _____
   _____

2. _____
   _____

3. _____
   _____

4. _____
   _____

B. **Directions:** Use the clues to complete the crossword puzzle. The answers are things you may have never seen or noticed.

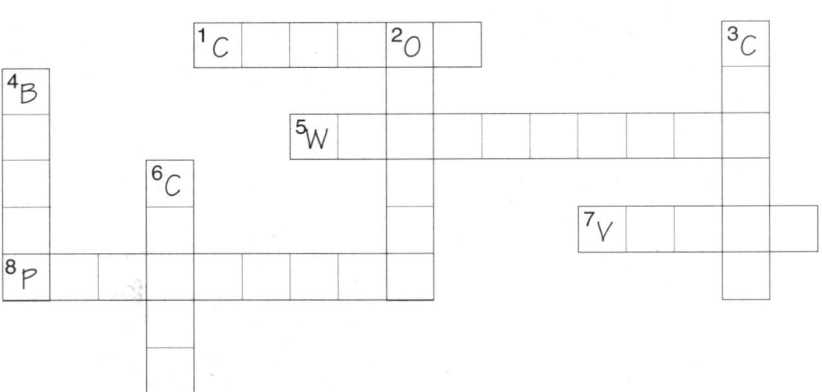

ACROSS

1. a long, narrow valley with high, rocky sides; often has a stream running through it

5. a movable chair on wheels, used by sick or injured people

7. planet sometimes called the "evening star"

8. a line of high cliffs, usually along a river

DOWN

2. the largest bodies of salt water on the face of the earth

3. a traveling show featuring clowns, trained animals, and acrobats

4. an airship shaped somewhat like an egg

6. high, steep face of rock that rises sharply from a shoreline

Name: _____   **Date:** _____

Observing your world also means "seeing" organizations, processes, and events—especially your government.

Directions: Write a letter to match each **boldface** word with its definition.

1. _____ **cabinet**

2. _____ **city manager**

3. _____ **committee**

4. _____ **election**

5. _____ **government**

6. _____ **governor**

7. _____ **legislature**

8. _____ **mayor**

9. _____ **organization**

10. _____ **representative**

11. _____ **senator**

a. chief government administrator of a state, province, territory, etc.

b. a group of people organized for some purpose

c. official organization that controls the affairs of a country, city, etc.

d. the head of government of a city or town

e. a group of people who meet to make laws for a country or state; example: the U.S. Congress

f. in the U.S. government, one of two people elected to represent each state in Congress

g. a group of people appointed by a larger group to study some matter or to accomplish a certain goal

h. the process of voting to choose candidates or decide issues

i. the chief administrator of a city or town

j. a group of officials who act as advisors to the head of a nation

k. in the U.S. government, a person elected by people in a district within a state to represent their district in Congress

Name: _____

Date: _____

Let's learn some facts about the states of our grand nation.

A. Directions: Use the clues to complete the crossword puzzle.

ACROSS

2. one of the states that borders the Mississippi River

5. the state that is separated from Mexico by the Rio Grande

8. the westernmost state

9. the state that is home to the Grand Canyon

10. the northernmost state on the Pacific shore

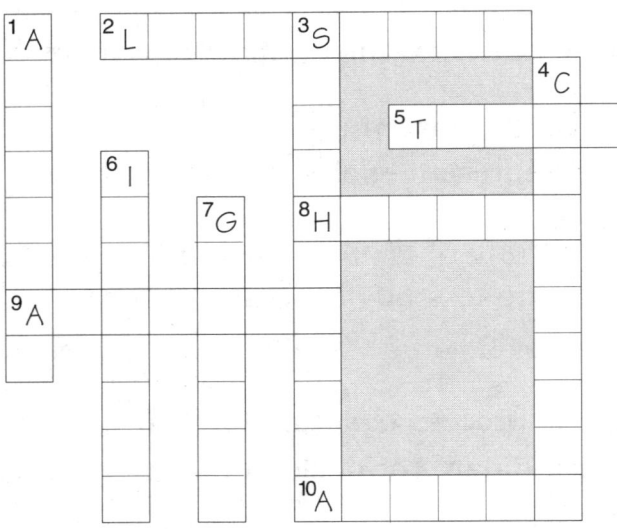

DOWN

1. the state that was home to President Bill Clinton before he became president

3. the state that is home to Mount Rushmore (2 words)

4. the state where Presidents Nixon and Reagan both retired

6. Chicago is in this state.

7. President Jimmy Carter came from and retired to this state.

B. Directions: Write two original sentences describing your own state.

1. _____

_____

2. _____

_____

Name: _____ **Date:** _____

And now let's learn some interesting facts about the rest of the world.

Directions: Use the clues to complete the crossword puzzle.

ACROSS

1. country on the west coast of Africa, founded by freed U.S. slaves
6. the South American home of the Incas
7. Middle Eastern country, east of Israel; ruled by a monarchy
8. African nation, the last country listed in the dictionary
11. country in which a huge Mardi Gras is celebrated in the city of Rio de Janeiro
12. referred to as "down under," this is both a country and a continent in the Southern Hemisphere
13. island nation in the North Atlantic

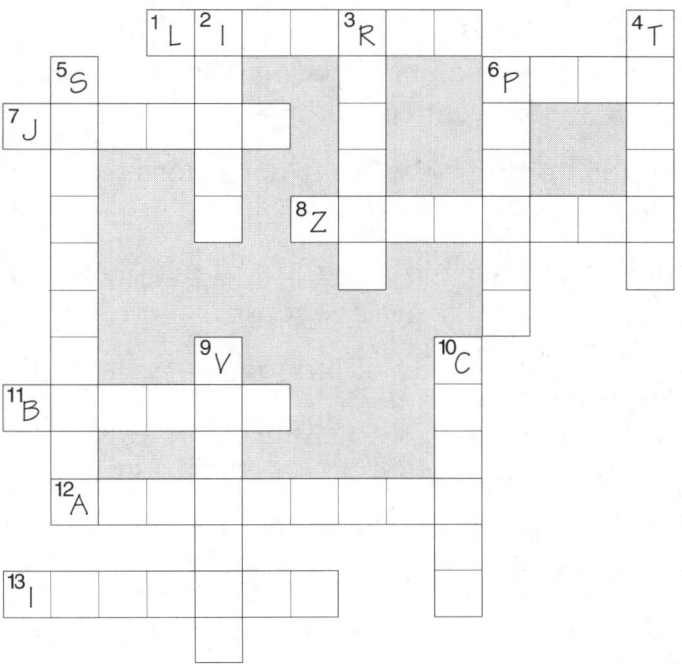

DOWN

2. home to the Coliseum, the canals of Venice, and pizza
3. one of the largest countries that once made up the Union of Socialist Soviet Republics (USSR)
4. a country lying mostly in western Asia, but partly in southeastern Europe
5. where the U.S. fought a controversial war ("police action") against North Korea and China in the 1950s (2 words)
6. Central American home to the canal connecting the Gulf of Mexico and the Pacific Ocean
9. where U.S. troops fought a controversial war in the '60s and '70s
10. U.S. neighbor to the north

Name: _____   **Date:** _____

Talk about *variety*! *Anthropology* is the scientific study of human beings—physical and cultural characteristics, distribution around the earth, social relationships, etc. Here are some terms describing different world cultures.

Directions: Write a letter to match each **boldface** word with its definition. Use a dictionary if you need help.

1. _____ **caste**
2. _____ **class**
3. _____ **culture**
4. _____ **customs**
5. _____ **dialect**
6. _____ **ethnic**
7. _____ **faith**
8. _____ **hierarchy**
9. _____ **linguistics**
10. _____ **religion**
11. _____ **rite**
12. _____ **superstition**
13. _____ **taboo**

a. a system of belief in God or a group of gods to be worshipped; often including moral ideals, philosophy of life, etc.

b. a belief or practice that rises from fear and ignorance; something generally considered irrational

c. any group in which there are higher and lower positions of power, rank, etc.

d. the way of life, including ideas, skills, arts, tools, etc., of a certain people at a certain time

e. things so often repeated that they have become the common or expected things to do

f. people grouped because of some likeness, usually economic or social

g. a system by which people are separated into classes because of their rank, wealth, etc.

h. unquestioning belief that does not require proof or evidence

i. adjective describing a group of people who have the same language, culture, etc.

j. the scientific study of language

k. the form of a language that is used only in a certain place or among a certain group

l. a religious or social practice that forbids doing certain things

m. a formal act or ceremony carried out according to fixed rules

Name: _____   **Date:** _____

Icons are images or pictures that represent certain things.

Directions: Complete the sentences with words from the box. Check a dictionary if you need help.

jai alai	dolmas	chopsticks	sari	Italian	Kwanzaa
lutefisk	serape	flamenco	obi	Irish	balalaika

1. When they dance the _____,
   Spanish dancers clap their hands and stamp their feet.

2. A Mexican _____ is a brightly
   colored woolen blanket worn as a cloak.

3. _____ are the preferred eating
   utensils used in some Asian countries.

4. A _____ is a Russian musical
   instrument that sounds much like a mandolin.

5. A Greek or Turkish specialty, _____
   are cabbage leaves stuffed with savory meat and rice.

6. Made of dried codfish preserved in lye, _____
   is always served at a Scandinavian smorgasbord.

7. The traditional dress worn by women of India is called a _____.

8. In an _____ step dance, the feet and legs move, but the arms
   and upper body do not.

9. The *tarantella* is a fast, whirling _____ folk dance.

10. The wide sash worn with a Japanese kimono is called an _____.

11. _____ is a game like handball that is very popular in
    Latin America.

12. The African-American festival of _____ gets its name
    from the Swahili language.

Name: _____   **Date:** _____

Why do people have favorite words? Some people like what the word means (*chocolate*). Others like the sound of the word (*rococo*). Still others are proud of having learned a difficult word (*numismatist*). Why do you like some words better than others?

Directions: Ask some people—friends, teachers, or family members—about their favorite words. Then ask them to explain why they like their words. In the chart below, record that information for five words.

Favorite Word: **Explanation:**

1. _____   _____
                        _____
                        _____

2. _____   _____
                        _____
                        _____

3. _____   _____
                        _____
                        _____

4. _____   _____
                        _____
                        _____

5. _____   _____
                        _____
                        _____

elegant

eclair   *brilliant*   *diamond*   *FLAMBOYANT*

Name: _____   **Date:** _____

Directions: Now it's your turn. Choose five of your own favorite words. On the lines below, write the words and explain why you like them. Then use your word in an original sentence.

Favorite Word: **Explanation:**

1. _____   _____

                               _____

   SENTENCE: _____

                               _____

2. _____   _____

                               _____

   SENTENCE: _____

                               _____

3. _____   _____

                               _____

   SENTENCE: _____

                               _____

4. _____   _____

                               _____

   SENTENCE: _____

                               _____

5. _____   _____

                               _____

   SENTENCE: _____

                               _____

Name: _____   **Date:** _____

SCOPE & SEQUENCE

STUDENT	DICTIONARY	VOWEL SOUNDS	HOMOGRAPHS	SYLLABLES	PARTS OF SPEECH	PREFIXES/SUFFIXES	ABBREVIATIONS	SYNONYMS	ANTONYMS	EUPHEMISMS	SHADES OF MEANING	CATEGORIES	WORD CHOICE	CONTRACTIONS	IDIOMS	MALL WORDS	SPORTS WORDS	WEATHER WORDS	MUSIC WORDS	MONUMENTS/LANDMARKS

SCOPE & SEQUENCE

STUDENT	MONEY WORDS	SCHOOL WORDS	MEDICAL WORDS	INVENTIONS/DISCOVERIES	WORKING WORLD	ABC WORDS	DEF WORDS	GHI WORDS	JKL WORDS	MNO WORDS	PQR WORDS	ST WORDS	UV WORDS	WXYZ WORDS	WORD WIZARD	WORDS IN CONTEXT	THE WORLD AROUND YOU	U.S. STATES	WORLD CULTURES	FAVORITE WORDS

PAGE 6
A. 1. words
2. verbal
3. Nonverbal
4. gestures
5. facial expressions
6. emphasize
7. frown
8. intonation
9. raising your eyebrows
10. smirk
11. shrug
B. Sentences will vary.

PAGE 7
A. 1. T, reading
2. F, spell
3. T, grammar
4. T, punctuation
5. T, uppercase
6. F, pronounce
7. F, alphabet
8. T, recognize
B. Circle: books, hieroglyphics, term papers, fliers, magazines, Internet Web pages, business letters, newspapers

PAGE 8
A. 1. friend   5. leave
2. mother   6. exactly!
3. money   7. informer
4. food   8. police officer
B. 1. control   5. much
2. clear   6. sassy
3. tasty   7. dull
4. passed   8. vague

PAGE 9
1. q   9. e   17. r
2. g   10. s   18. d
3. t   11. c   19. m
4. o   12. f   20. l
5. u   13. h   21. b
6. i   14. v   22. n
7. k   15. j
8. p   16. a

PAGE 10
A. 1. antibody   6. neutron
2. estimate   7. preview
3. glory   8. satisfy
4. likely   9. tangible
5. motorize   10. upbraid
B. 1. earache   6. empower
2. ebb   7. entire
3. edge   8. estimate
4. eleven   9. excite
5. embody   10. eyebrow

PAGE 11
A. 1. place   6. pledge
2. plague   7. plow
3. plank   8. plumbing
4. playoff   9. plural
5. plead   10. plywood
B. Answers will vary.

PAGE 12
A SOUNDS
1. clasp   2. weigh
   plaque   plate
   task   gait
E SOUNDS
1. vest   2. seam
   bread   plead
   fresh   creep
I SOUNDS
1. fiddle   2. pint
   miss   thigh
   stitch   shy
O SOUNDS
1. shock   2. clothes
   oxen   boat
   odd   logo
U SOUNDS
1. tough   2. through
   much   glue
   bunk   brew

PAGE 13
A. CROSS OUT:
1. law, table
2. were, legal
3. lion, rifle
4. product, olive
5. bushy, study
B. 1. allow   5. noun
2. short   6. short
3. plays   7. cheer
4. long

PAGE 14
Original sentences will vary.
1. deepen
2. soothe (or seethe)
3. goodness
4. seethe (or soothe)
5. disagree
6. childhood
7. misdeed
8. freely
9. oodles
10. rookie
11. wheedle
12. proof

PAGE 15
ACROSS: 4. meddle   5. occult
6. sallow   7. summit
8. Mississippi   9. Tennessee
11. annals   12. immemorial
DOWN: 1. belligerent   2. immense
3. illuminate   6. successor
7. satellite   10. pallid

PAGE 16
Sentences will vary.

PAGE 17
A. 1. c   5. d   9. g   13. d
2. g   6. e   10. b   14. a
3. b   7. a   11. f   15. g
4. e   8. f   12. c
B. Word choices and sentences will vary.

PAGE 18
A. 1. brow•beat   4. spite•ful
2. e•lapse   5. sys•tem
3. mis•judge   6. u•nique
B. 1. d   3. f   5. g   7. e
2. a   4. h   6. c   8. b
C. Circle: rustproof, exhume, malign, trademark, mammal, wheedle, seclude

PAGE 19
A. 1. a•bun•dant
2. clum•si•ness
3. mil•lion•aire
4. prob•i•ty
5. syn•thet•ic
6. ve•he•ment
B. 1. c   3. f   5. b   7. h
2. e   4. g   6. d   8. a
C. Circle: eyeglasses, disbelief, pseudonym, aboveboard, tarpaulin, localize, glandular

PAGE 20
A. ACROSS: 2. platter
5. mangle   6. utter
8. gravy   9. saucer
11. masher
DOWN: 1. mobster
3. treasure   4. rip-off
7. oyster   10. hazy
B. Sentences will vary.

PAGE 21
A. Sentences will vary.
B. 1. levity   6. president
2. edible   7. saturate
3. extensive   8. pathetic
4. ovation   9. reverence
5. religious   10. numeral

PAGE 22
A. Circle: vehicle, velvet, Golden Gate Bridge, sinew, dawn, vegetable, horse, Eiffel Tower
B. Sentences will vary.

PAGE 23
A. Circle: multimillionaire, vassal, judge, diplomat, New Orleans, athlete, President Bush, plumber, pedagogue, engraver
B. Sentences will vary.

PAGE 24
1. are
2. gives
3. take
4. behave
5. enjoys
6. look
7. is
8. Can, lend
9. are, coming
10. Do, participate

PAGE 25
A. 1. N   3. F   5. N
2. P   4. P
B. 1. judged
2. will celebrate
3. was reviled
4. aspire
5. convened
6. will embarrass
C. Sentences will vary.

PAGE 26
1. Zeke's
2. hardest
3. red, red
4. long, hot
5. romaine
6. Victorian
7. centennial
8. horror
9. heavy metal
10. Shakespeare

PAGE 27
A. 2. disorganized
3. boring
4. contagious
5. delicious (or sweet)
6. sweet (or delicious)
7. burly
8. terrifying
B. Sentences will vary.

PAGE 28
1. inadvertently
2. radically
3. harmoniously
4. urgently
5. beautifully
6. handily
7. randomly
8. squarely
9. spitefully
10. casually

PAGE 29
A. Most likely answers, but some variations possible:
1. simply
2. devoutly
3. courageously
4. immensely
5. very
B. Sentences will vary.

PAGE 30
2. stepfather
3. DVD player
4. motorcycles
5. Isabel
6. videotapes
7. city council
8. sang
9. fence
10. interesting

PAGE 31
A. 1. she is hoarse
2. he wants to graduate
3. they were extremely harsh
4. no one fails the test
5. she can play in the band
6. you missed the field trip
7. he could get his GED
8. they drive all night
B. Sentence conclusions will vary.

PAGE 32
1. fraud
2. sports
3. drugs
4. junk food
5. family
6. detention
7. music
8. pollution
9. war

PAGE 33
A. 1. to mess things up
2. to take something apart
3. to make someone lose hope
4. a feeling against something
5. to hurt someone's reputation
6. to legally take something away
7. to vanish from sight
8. to take away someone's ability
9. to deny
B. Sentences will vary.

PAGE 34
A. 1. dancing
2. giving
3. diving
4. bowling
5. eating
6. shouting
7. offering
8. Talking (or Sleeping)
9. waking
10. Sleeping (or Talking)
B. Sentences will vary.

PAGE 35
A. 2. fluctuates
3. concentrate
4. deliberated
5. speculate
6. generate
7. separate
8. stipulates
B. 1. capitalize
2. publicized
3. personalize
4. idolize
5. sympathize

PAGE 36
A. 1. card
2. part
3. egg
4. batch
5. box
6. sign
7. truth
8. stress
9. church
10. report
B. Sentences will vary.

PAGE 37
A. 1. oxen
2. children
3. halves
4. wolves
5. calves
6. feet
7. arroyos
8. salvos, salvoes
9. tornados, tornadoes
10. geese
11. moose
12. bison
13. mice
14. potatoes
15. tomatoes
16. teeth
B. Sentences will vary.

PAGE 38
A. 1. superintendent
2. master of ceremonies
3. doctor of medicine
4. police department
5. milligram(s)
6. foot or feet
7. in care of
8. boulevard
B. ACROSS: 3. pair
7. touchdown 8. chapter
DOWN: 1. mile 2. pronoun
3. postscript 4. and so forth 5. brothers
6. company

PAGE 39
A. 1. Massachusetts
2. Nebraska
3. Connecticut
4. Virginia
5. Texas
6. Nevada
7. California
8. Arizona
9. Michigan
10. Florida
11. Alabama
12. Maine
B. 1. Nebraska
2. Arizona
3. Florida
4. Michigan
5. Alabama
6. Nevada
7. Massachusetts
8. Virginia
9. Maine
10. California
11. Texas
12. Connecticut

PAGE 40
A. 1. MADD
2. scuba
3. KISS
4. FEMA
5. BASIC
6. WYSIWYG
7. radar
8. SARS
9. UNESCO
10. AIDS
B. Sentences will vary but should include proper use of the following acronyms:
1. SWAK: sealed with a kiss
2. sonar: sound navigation and ranging
3. SAT: Scholastic Assessment (or Aptitude) Test

PAGE 41
A. 1. Mrs.
2. Mr.
3. Miss
4. Ms.
5. Maj.
6. Col.
7. Sgt.
8. P.F.C.
B. 1. President
2. District Attorney
3. Professor
4. Governor
5. Doctor
6. Licensed Practical Nurse

PAGE 42
A. 1. glory
2. catastrophe
3. visage
4. orderly
5. system
6. recuperate
7. suppose
8. complain
9. aspire
B. Answers will vary. Possible answers:
1. prisoner
2. miniature
3. diverse
4. eject
5. probable
6. dwelling
7. dusk
8. logical
9. gigantic
10. pressing

PAGE 43
A. Answers will vary. Possible synonyms used in sentences:
1. odor, perfume
2. tired, weak, worn out
3. quarrel, fight
4. schedule
5. selfish, stingy
6. dangerous, daring
B. ACROSS: 2. zero 4. fake
5. dress 7. false
8. wealth 9. fire
DOWN: 1. canoe 3. rural
5. dear 6. step

PAGE 44
A. 1. c 4. b 7. h
2. a 5. f 8. e
3. d 6. g
B. 1. evil
2. relaxing
3. dismantled
4. spicy
5. expand
6. graceful
7. pride

PAGE 45
A. Sequence will vary.
1. backward / forward
2. congenial / hostile
3. critic / fan
4. diverse / similar
5. dawn / sunset
6. dependent / independent
7. starved / fed
8. joy / sorrow
B. ACROSS: 2. open 5. dismal
7. far 8. empty
DOWN: 1. few 2. ordinary
3. speedy 4. plump
6. male

PAGE 46
A. 1. d 4. b 7. h
2. c 5. g 8. e
3. a 6. f
B. 1. never
2. bad-tempered
3. lazy
4. apathy
5. irrational
6. dry
7. friends

PAGE 47
A. Sequence will vary.
1. leave / return
2. mirth / sadness
3. fop / slob
4. pitch / catch
5. deluge / drought
6. hyper / mellow
7. indifferent / eager
8. exclusive / inclusive
B. ACROSS: 2. safety
3. confirm 4. wide
6. rough 7. sweet
DOWN: 1. mend 2. straight
5. sober

PAGE 48
A. 2. A, S, C
3. C, S, A
4. C, S, A
5. A, C, S
6. S, A, C
7. C, S, A
8. S, A, C
B. Answers will vary.

PAGE 49

A. 2. trickle
brook
river
3. OK
good
excellent
perfect
4. tiny
small
medium
large
huge
5. pond
sea
ocean
6. cool
chilly
cold
freezing

B. Answers will vary. Possible answers:
1. Hawaii is much warmer than the North Pole.
2. A hill is much smaller than a mountain.
3. A handkerchief is much softer than sandpaper.

PAGE 50

A. 1. passed away
2. visually impaired
3. a senior citizen
4. maintenance engineers
5. adult

B. 1. crippled
2. crazy
3. dump
4. trounced
5. died
6. bossy
7. quit
8. victim
9. use the bathroom
10. fat
11. problem
12. used

PAGE 51

Sentences will vary.

PAGE 52

A. 2. as strong as an ox
3. as sharp as a tack
4. as grumpy as a bear
5. as pretty as a picture
6. as bold as brass

B. Answers will vary.

PAGE 53

A. Answers will vary.

B. 1. a wet hen
2. a cat on a hot tin roof
3. an eel
4. a gorilla
5. a kitten
6. a lamb

C. Answers will vary.

PAGE 54

A. 2. rustic, rural
3. walk, stroll
4. help, assist
5. harm, injure

B. 1. furious
2. possesses
3. governs
4. wished I could

C. Answers will vary.

PAGE 55

A. 1. d   5. i   9. e
2. k   6. c   10. g
3. a   7. j   11. b
4. f   8. l   12. h

B. **ACROSS:** 4. important
5. brief   7. dry   8. permit
9. gaze
DOWN: 1. melted   2. many
3. forbid   4. itemized
6. burning

PAGE 56

A. 1. weigh, whey
2. align, divine
3. thrill, fulfill
4. meditation, imitation
5. hesitate, confiscate
6. off, trough
7. prim, gym
8. train, reign

B. **CIRCLE:** open, bow, whole, hope, dough, poll, cold, suppose, hallow

C. Answers will vary.

PAGE 57

A. 1. (pr)ide
2. ~~reign~~
3. (fr)ight
4. ~~shoe~~
5. ~~collide~~
6. ~~might~~
7. ~~align~~
8. (cr)i(sp)
9. ~~jury~~
10. (str)aight
11. ~~shallow~~
12. quai(nt)

B. **ACROSS:** 3. brand   4. plaid
6. greed   7. cord   8. wide
9. end
DOWN: 1. trade   2. said
4. parade   5. seed

PAGE 58

A. 1. b   5. l   9. h
2. c   6. p   10. e
3. k   7. i   11. o
4. g   8. a   12. j

B. Answers will vary.

PAGE 59

A. 2. holes in the ground
3. objects in space
4. colors
5. happy things; having a good time
6. forms of transportation
7. funny things
8. shrubs or bushes
9. bad or unhappy feelings
10. things to write with— specifically, pens

B. Answers will vary.

PAGE 60

A. 1. transparent
2. physician
3. implying
4. pemmican
5. secede
6. attain

B. 2. gleam
3. row
4. crux
5. contraction

PAGE 61

1. l   8. d   15. q
2. s   9. r   16. e
3. a   10. c   17. f
4. j   11. o   18. g
5. b   12. p   19. n
6. i   13. t   20. h
7. k   14. m

PAGE 62

A. 1. should've
2. don't
3. Shepherd's
4. don't, won't
5. I'm, you've
6. Gene'll, he'll
7. should've

B. 2. I would
3. Sherri has
4. judge will
5. sheriff has
6. deputy is
7. They have
8. they had
9. did not
10. I am

PAGE 63

A. 1. He'd
2. shouldn't
3. I've
4. friends'll
5. Jonah's
6. must've
7. She's
8. I'll

B. Sentences will vary.

PAGE 64

A. 2. plumb
3. quack
4. Strangers
5. Vicki
6. half
7. recite
8. clowns

B. **ACROSS:** 2. ladder   5. idle
6. tummy   7. rangers
8. spiteful
DOWN: 1. pronounce
3. precious   4. cymbals

PAGE 65

2. Please park your motorcycle in the driveway.
3. Some men in the Middle East wear turbans.
4. My grandmother used to operate a switchboard.
5. Brad's ankle was very swollen after the accident.
6. Many people use swivel chairs at their desks.
7. A relic is something that remains from the past.
8. It's a relief to be home after such a long trip.
9. Our argument finally reached an impasse.
10. The sport of fencing is not taught at many schools.

PAGE 66

A. 2. She   4. there
3. them   5. It

B. 2. 1, 2   5. 2, 1
3. 2, 1   6. 2, 1
4. 1, 2

C. 2. C   4. C
3. I   5. I

PAGE 67
1. I have an aunt named Elvira. She lives in Buffalo, New York. The weather there is harsh in the winter.
2. Dave wanted to be an architect. To do that, he had to do well in math, drawing, and science. Unfortunately, his grades in those subjects were poor.
3. This is the recipe for stuffed cabbage: Purchase some cabbage, rice, hamburger, and tomato sauce. Cook the rice and cabbage leaves. Combine the cooked rice with the hamburger. Wrap the combination in the cabbage leaves. Cover the stuffed cabbage with tomato sauce. Bake in the oven.
4. Why learn new words? The more words you know, the more brain power you have. The more brain power you have, the more confidence you have. The more confidence you have, the better your life will be.

PAGE 68
A. 1. b   4. c   7. g
   2. f   5. a
   3. e   6. d
B. 1. a   3. a   5. a
   2. c   4. b

PAGE 69
1. held down
2. on hold
3. Hold on
4. hold up
5. holdup
6. holding out
7. held off
8. held back
9. held forth
10. held over

PAGE 70
A. 1. c   4. e   7. b
   2. g   5. d   8. f
   3. h   6. a
B. 1. c   3. c   5. b
   2. b   4. a

PAGE 71
1. let your hair down
2. split hairs
3. hairsbreadth
4. hairspring
5. hairline
6. hairpiece
7. hairy (or hair-raising)
8. hairpin
9. hairdo
10. hair-raising (or hairy)

PAGE 72
A. 1. e   5. a or d
   2. b   6. a or d
   3. f   7. c
   4. g   8. h
B. 1. passed up
   2. came to pass
   3. passed over
   4. passed out
   5. passed away

PAGE 73
1. stand up
2. stand a chance
3. stand out
4. stand up to
5. stand by
6. stand up
7. stand in for
8. stand by
9. stand for
10. stand off

PAGE 74
A. 1. d   4. h   7. b
   2. e   5. a   8. c
   3. g   6. f
B. 1. pull off
   2. pull over
   3. pull for
   4. pull through
   5. pull your leg

PAGE 75
1. b   5. c   9. c
2. a   6. b   10. b
3. c   7. b
4. a   8. a

PAGE 76
ACROSS: 4. parking lot
   6. atrium   8. window shop
   9. sales clerk   11. purchase
   14. fountain   15. hang out
   16. beauty shop
DOWN: 1. manager
   2. shopping center
   3. browse   5. food court
   7. merchandise   10. bench
   12. open air   13. kiosk

PAGE 77
1. atrium
2. hang out
3. merchandise
4. sales clerk
5. bench
6. manager
7. kiosk
8. food court
9. browse
10. window shop
11. shopping center

PAGE 78
ACROSS: 1. match   3. stadium
   5. quarter   6. rally
   9. racquet   12. touchdown
   13. rink   14. pep
DOWN: 2. court   3. set
   4. marathon   7. love
   8. half-time   10. inning
   11. jock

PAGE 79
1. pep rally
2. marathon
3. touchdown
4. match, love
5. half-time
6. court
7. stadium
8. quarter
9. racquet
10. inning
11. rink

PAGE 80
ACROSS: 1. windstorm
   3. atmosphere   6. cloudburst
   9. tempest   11. tsunami
   12. typhoon   14. hurricane
DOWN: 2. tornado   4. monsoon
   5. humidity   7. temperature
   8. barometer   9. tidal wave
   10. cyclone   13. hail

PAGE 81
1. barometer
2. humidity
3. monsoon
4. temperature
5. tsunami or tidal wave
6. Tempest
7. hurricane
8. tornado
9. hail
10. windstorm
11. cyclones

PAGE 82
ACROSS: 5. duet   7. stringed
   8. orchestra   9. soloist
   13. brass   14. woodwind
   15. conductor   16. ensemble
DOWN: 1. musician   2. concert
   3. quartet   4. performance
   6. percussion   10. trio
   11. band   12. debut

PAGE 83
1. conductor
2. percussion
3. brass
4. duet
5. orchestra
6. debut
7. performance
8. concert
9. woodwind
10. stringed
11. quartet

PAGE 84
A. 1. b   4. e   7. d
   2. g   5. c   8. a
   3. h   6. f
B. Sentences will vary.

PAGE 85
A. 1. e   4. g   7. c
   2. f   5. h   8. b
   3. d   6. a
B. Sentences will vary.

PAGE 86
A. 1. e   5. c   9. j
   2. g   6. f   10. h
   3. d   7. i
   4. b   8. a
B. 1. teller
   2. savings
   3. your money's worth
   4. credit card
   5. check

PAGE 87
A. 1. money-changer
   2. bank cards
   3. money order
   4. on the money
   5. moneybags
   6. money belt
B. Sentences will vary.

PAGE 88
ACROSS: 4. liberal arts
   8. middle   10. kindergarten
   11. master's   12. university
   13. degree   14. community
   15. scholarship
DOWN: 1. college   2. trade
   3. elementary   5. tuition
   6. diploma   7. junior high
   9. bachelor's

PAGE 89
1. Elementary
2. kindergarten
3. middle
4. community
5. trade
6. master's
7. diploma
8. degree
9. scholarship
10. tuition

PAGE 90
ACROSS: 1. technician
5. nurse   11. physician
12. laboratory
13. intensive care unit
14. blood pressure
15. disease
DOWN: 2. emergency room
3. hospital   4. health
6. symptom   7. ambulance
8. pulse   9. clinic
10. diagnosis

PAGE 91
1. physician
2. Clinic
3. nurse
4. hospital
5. ambulance
6. emergency room
7. symptom
8. diagnosis
9. technician
10. laboratory
11. health

PAGE 92
A. 1. l   6. g   11. e
2. k   7. f   12. c
3. j   8. m   13. h
4. b   9. n   14. i
5. d   10. a
B. Sentences will vary.

PAGE 93
1. South Pole
2. radium
3. penicillin
4. North Pole
5. Pacific Ocean
6. "new world"
7. Halley's Comet
8. the Hawaiian Islands
9. trade route
10. Cape of Good Hope

PAGE 94
ACROSS: 2. interview
5. candidate   8. supervisor
9. counselor   11. screen
12. trainee   13. aptitude
14. sick leave
DOWN: 1. human resources
3. retirement   4. wages
6. annual leave   7. résumé
8. salary   10. intern

PAGE 95
1. résumé
2. interview
3. human resources
4. intern
5. sick leave
6. annual leave
7. supervisor
8. counselors
9. aptitude
10. candidates
11. screens

PAGE 96
ACROSS: 5. drive
7. convertible   8. manual
10. transmission
11. automatic
13. unleaded   14. power
DOWN: 1. octane   2. brakes
3. steering   4. sidewall
6. minivan   7. classic
9. pickup   12. make

PAGE 97
1. classic
2. brakes
3. minivan
4. unleaded
5. automatic
6. steering
7. pickup
8. convertible
9. sidewalls
10. make
11. octane

PAGE 98
A. 1. stop work as a protest
2. become speechless
3. have a desired effect
4. suddenly become wealthy
5. cross out something on a list
6. get three strikes in baseball
7. start something
8. make a coin
9. take down or take apart a camp
B. Sentences will vary.

PAGE 99
A. 1. badly confuse someone
2. deliberately lose
3. vomit
4. give up
5. get rid of it
6. quickly prepare something
7. misbehave out of anger
8. like a primitive type
9. turn it on or off
B. Sentences will vary.

PAGE 100
1. venal
2. quash
3. shenanigans
4. aggravate
5. caterpillar
6. rival
7. dreary
8. yolk

PAGE 101
Sentences will vary.

PAGE 102
2. h   6. i   10. a
3. k   7. d   11. c
4. l   8. b   12. g
5. j   9. f

PAGE 103
A. Sentences will vary.
B. Topic words and sentences will vary.

PAGE 104
1. bedrock   7. boast
2. chimpanzee   8. aquarium
3. astonish   9. carpenter
4. crease   10. conclusive
5. blemish   11. bunkhouse
6. advocate   12. almanac

PAGE 105
A. Sentences will vary.
B. Words and descriptions will vary.

PAGE 106
1. elegy   7. excavate
2. fervent   8. fragile
3. diligent   9. faulty
4. embassy   10. dainty
5. eavesdrop   11. flatter
6. douse   12. deadlocked

PAGE 107
A. Sentences will vary.
B. Words and descriptions will vary.

PAGE 108
1. grasp   7. horizon
2. hypocrite   8. indistinct
3. hacker   9. illegible
4. Itinerant   10. heliport
5. gall   11. gimmick
6. impersonal   12. goad

PAGE 109
A. Sentences will vary.
B. Words and descriptions will vary.

PAGE 110
1. karate   7. jeopardy
2. labyrinth   8. literal
3. knoll   9. killjoy
4. jabber   10. jealous
5. lozenge   11. kennel
6. leeway   12. judgment

PAGE 111
A. Sentences will vary.
B. Words and descriptions will vary.

PAGE 112
1. ointment
2. nincompoop
3. name-dropper
4. makeshift
5. overwrought
6. ostracize
7. oath
8. nutrition
9. megaphone
10. nostalgia
11. muscle
12. mischievous

PAGE 113
A. Sentences will vary.
B. Words and descriptions will vary.

PAGE 114
1. preliminary   7. pedal
2. ruddy   8. quibble
3. quadrant   9. quartz
4. quilt   10. plumage
5. ransom   11. panhandle
6. rebound   12. routine

PAGE 115
A. Sentences will vary.
B. Words and descriptions will vary.

PAGE 116
1. tambourine
2. smorgasbord
3. sham
4. thwart
5. shawl
6. transcribe
7. Thin-skinned
8. tumble
9. squall
10. telethon
11. serene
12. singe

PAGE 117
A. Sentences will vary.
B. Words and descriptions will vary.

PAGE 118
1. unearth   7. upholstery
2. vacant   8. vacillate
3. vindictive   9. unbiased
4. unsightly   10. valiant
5. ventilate   11. vouch
6. ultimatum   12. utopia

PAGE 119
A. Sentences will vary.
B. Words and descriptions will vary.

PAGE 120
1. zucchini   7. X-ray
2. wound   8. yearn
3. yuletide   9. Xenon
4. weary   10. yacht
5. zoology   11. wary
6. zealous   12. xylophone

PAGE 121
A. Sentences will vary.
B. Words and descriptions will vary.

PAGE 122
Sentences will vary.

PAGE 123
Sentences will vary.

PAGE 124
Sentences will vary.

PAGE 125
Sentences will vary.

PAGE 126

A. More Physical: calisthenics, combat, fencing, polo, rodeo, scull, stampede, waterskiing

Less Physical: basking, cribbage, darning, editing, mahjong, daydreaming, orating, patching

B. ACROSS: 3. combat
7. mahjong 8. rodeo
DOWN: 1. scull
2. stampede 4. basking
5. cribbage 6. polo

PAGE 127

A. Circle: deliberate, envision, reminisce, imagine, meditate, contemplate, recollect, reflect, ponder, scrutinize, consider, ruminate, brood, fantasize, visualize
B. Sentences will vary.

PAGE 128

A. Sentences will vary.
B. ACROSS: 1. canyon
5. wheelchair 7. Venus
8. palisades
DOWN: 2. oceans 3. circus
4. blimp 6. cliff

PAGE 129

1. j   5. c   9. b
2. i   6. a   10. k
3. g   7. e   11. f
4. h   8. d

PAGE 130

A. ACROSS: 2. Louisiana
5. Texas 8. Hawaii
9. Arizona 10. Alaska
DOWN: 1. Arkansas
3. South Dakota
4. California 6. Illinois
7. Georgia
B. Sentences will vary.

PAGE 131

ACROSS: 1. Liberia 6. Peru
7. Jordan 8. Zimbabwe
11. Brazil 12. Australia
13. Iceland
DOWN: 2. Italy 3. Russia
4. Turkey 5. South Korea
6. Panama 9. Vietnam
10. Canada

PAGE 132

1. g   6. i   11. m
2. f   7. h   12. b
3. d   8. c   13. l
4. e   9. j
5. k   10. a

PAGE 133

1. flamenco
2. serape
3. Chopsticks
4. balalaika
5. dolmas
6. lutefisk
7. sari
8. Irish
9. Italian
10. obi
11. Jai alai
12. Kwanzaa

PAGE 134

Answers will vary.

PAGE 135

Answers will vary.